The Persian '*Ma*
The Zoroastrian 'Book of the Snake' Omens & Calendar

By Payam Nabarz

and

The Old Iranian Calender

By S H Taqizadeh

The Persian *'Mar Nameh'*:
The Zoroastrian 'Book of the Snake' Omens & Calendar

By Dr. Payam Nabarz © 2006. All rights reserved.
Published by Twin Serpents Limited 2006

10 digit ISBN 1–905524–25–0
13 digit ISBN 978–1–905524–25–9

Copyright Part 1 and Appendix © 2006 Dr Payam Nabarz

Permission for the publication of Dr Taqizadeh's essay was kindly given by Joseph H. Peterson, and The Royal Asiatic Society.

Includes bibliographic references.

Printed on acid-free paper.

All rights reserved.

This book is published for information purposes only. Twin Serpents Limited and their autors and affiliated parties accept no liability for any consequences of use of the information described in this book.

This book is sold subject to the conditions that it shall not, by way of trade or otherwise, be lent, resold, hired out, or otherwise circulated without the publisher's prior consent in any form of binding or cover other than that in which it is published and without a similar condition including this condition being imposed upon the subsequent purchase.
No Copyright part of this book may be reproduced or utilized in any form or by any means, electronic or mechanical, including photocopying, recording, or by any information storage or retrieval system, without permission in writing from the publisher.

Direct all enquiries through:

www.twinserpents.com

Table of contents

Acknowledgements 4

Part 1
Chapter 1. Introduction 5
Chapter 2. Mar Nameh (the transliteration) 16
Chapter 3 Persian Text of Mar Nameh 19
Chapter 4 Mar Nameh (the translation) 27
Chapter 5. Spirit of the days and their meaning ... 30
Sirozas: Prayer and dedications for the thirty days of the month 33
Siroza 1 33
Siroza 2 38
Bibliography 44
Further Readings 45

Part 2
The Old Iranian Calendars 48
Notes 86
Biographies 101

Appendix
The Gregorian calendar conversion to the Persian calendar 102
Calendar year 2006 conversion to Zoroastrian calendar year 3743 102
Calendar year 2007 conversion to Zoroastrian calendar year 3744 111
Calendar year 2008 conversion to Zoroastrian calendar year 3745 120

By the same author.
The Mysteries of Mithras: The Pagan Belief That Shaped the Christian World.
Inner Traditions, 2005.
http://www.innertraditions.com/isbn/1-59477-027-1

Acknowledgements
To Alison Jones for reading of this manuscript and her numerous helpful comments and discussions.
To John H for his helpful comments.
To Nigel S (Twin Serpents) for the very helpful numerous editorial comments.
I would like to thank my dear father for the Persian calligraphy in chapter 3. Khily manon pader azizam.

Every effort has been made to trace holders of copyrights. Any inadvertent omissions of acknowledgement or permission will be rectified in future editions.

CHAPTER 1 – INTRODUCTION

"Theopomus (born c. 380 B.C.) says that, according to the Magians, for three thousand years alternatively the one god will dominate the other and be dominated, and that for another three thousand years they will fight and make war, until one smashes up the domain of the other. In the end Hades (Ahriman) shall perish and men shall be happy; neither shall they need sustenance nor shall they cast a shadow, while the god who will have brought this about shall have quiet and shall rest, not for a long while indeed for a god, but for such time as would be reasonable for a man who falls asleep. Such is the mythology of the Magians." (*Plurarch's De Iside et Osiride*, as translated by J.Gwyn Griffiths [1]).

The snake enters the Biblical epic of the Fall of humanity by offering Eve the apple of knowledge. The result of eating it is described as awareness of our true self *"For God doth know that in the day ye eat thereof, then your eyes shall be opened, and ye shall be as gods, knowing good and evil."* Gen3:5.

Before the Fall, mankind is said to have been in paradise in a state of bliss as immortal, where there was no aging or death. Indeed, Adam is told to not eat from tree of knowledge as it would lead to his death. *"But of the tree of the knowledge of good and evil, thou shalt not eat of it: for in the day that thou eatest thereof thou shalt surely die."* Gen2:17.

The snake defeats Adam and Eve by not attacking or killing them directly, but rather causing them to become mortal and die from old age. The serpent's act essentially brings humankind and all life from the Biblical paradise into a linear time, where all are born and die. The connection between snake and time is seen in other mythologies too. For example, in Hinduism Lord Shiva is often shown with a snake (Vasuki) curled three times around his neck representing past, present, and future cycles of time.

[**Figure:** Shiva. Lord Shiva with a snake curled three times around his neck. Painting by unknown artist.]

Lord Shiva wears time symbolizing that while creation is time dependent, he is beyond time. In Hinduism there is also 'Anata' meaning 'Endless, infinite'; the name of the world snake on which Visnu lies in his form as Anantasayana. The alchemical symbol of the Ouroboros, snake swallowing its own tail is said to represent the wheel of time, constantly renewing itself.

In Mithraism too, we see a snake curling around the body of the Mithraic 'God of Time' the Leontocephaline, a figure often described as Immortal Time and Aion. This figure is often linked to Zurvan the Persian God of Immortal time. This Mithraic Aion is also linked to the other gods of time Kronos and Saturn / Father Time. Its statues or paintings have always depicted it with a snake winding around it; it is standing on the cosmic sphere and holding a key in its right hand, and its body is often decorated with the signs of the zodiac and stars.

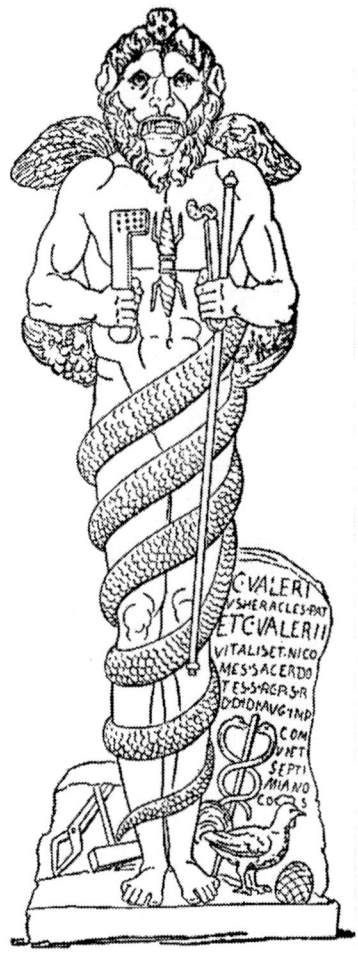

[**Figure:** The Leontocephaline: the Mithraic God of Time and Aion with the snake winding around it. (From *The Mysteries of Mithra*, by Franz Cumont. New York: Dover, 1956. [Originally published in 1903 by Open Court Publishing, London.])

The connection between snakes and time is seen in the myth of Chronos, the Greek god of time. In the Orphic poems he is described as a creative serpent emerging from water chaos. In the Orphic 'Rhapsodic Theogony', the cosmic egg is broken by the 'Serpent Time' coiling around the egg.

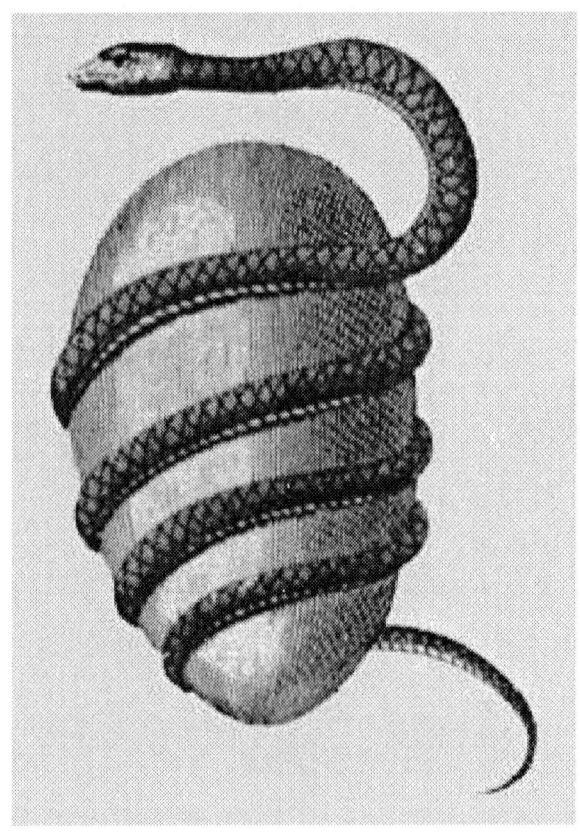

The egg is all of creation which becomes manifest once it is broken open. Interestingly, the snake and egg are also the symbols of Damballah the Voodoo god of fertility. We also see a central role for snakes in the Norse myths too, the world tree 'Yggdrasil' had at its base a great cosmic serpent that gnawed at its roots while guarding it.

In Islamic Hadith some snakes are described as Jinns (evil spirits); if someone sees a snake in their house, they should give it a warning three times over three days. If the snake returns after the warnings, they should kill it, for it is evil. Giving three warnings gives 'time' to the snake to escape.

The connection between the snake and time is seen in many mythologies, none more so than the Persian Zoroastrian *'Mar Nameh'*: The Book of the Snake. Here we see the battle between forces of Light (Ahura Mazda) and Darkness (Ahriman) is fought in 'Time'. The twin sons of Zurvan (the Immortal Time) battle for dominion over the worlds.

When nothing existed at all, neither heaven nor earth, the great god Zurvan (Infinite Time) alone existed, whose name means 'fate' or 'fortune'. He offered sacrifice for a thousand years that perchance he might have a son who should be called Ohrmazd (Ahura Mazda or Hormozd) and who would create heaven and earth. At the end of this period of a thousand years he began to ponder and said to himself: "What use is this sacrifice that I am offering, and will I really have a son called Ohrmazd, or am I taking all this trouble in vain?" And no sooner had this thought occurred to him then both Ohrmazd and Ahriman were conceived – Ohrmazd because of the sacrifice he had offered, and Ahriman because of his doubt. When he realized that there were two sons in the womb, he made a vow saying: "Whichever of the two shall come to me first, him will I make king." Ohrmazd was apprised of his father's thought and revealed it to Ahriman. When Ahriman heard this, he ripped the womb open, emerged, and advanced towards his father. Zurvan, seeing him, asked him: "Who art thou?" And he replied: "I am thy son, Ohrmazd." And Zurvan said: "My son is light and fragrant, but thou art dark and stinking." And he wept most bitterly. And as they were talking together, Ohrmazd was born in his turn, light and fragrant; and Zurvan, seeing him, knew that it was his son Ohrmazd for whom he had offered sacrifice. Taking the barsom twigs he held in his hands with which he had been sacrificing, he gave them to Ohrmazd and said: "Up till now it is I who have offered thee sacrifice; from now on shalt thou sacrifice to me." But even as Zurvan handed the sacrificial twigs to Ohrmazd, Ahriman drew near and said to him: "Didst thou not vow that whichever of the sons should come to thee first, to him wouldst thou give the kingdom?" And Zurvan said to him: "O false and wicked one, the kingdom shall be granted thee for nine thousand years, but Ohrmazd have I made a king above thee, and after nine thousand years he will reign and will do everything according to his good pleasure." And Ohrmazd created the heavens and the earth and all things that are beautiful and good; but Ahriman created the demons and all that is evil and perverse. Ohrmazd created riches, Ahriman poverty. – From the Persian Pahlavi text *circa* 300 AD. R.C. Zaehner, *The Dawn and Twilight of Zoroastrianism* [2].

The Persian poem *'Mar Nameh'* describes in verse what seeing a snake on every one of the 30 days of a month will mean and what omen it will portend. The thirty-two couplets in Persian lyrical rhyme and are part of the 'Parsee Revayats' prose and poem collection (15th – 18th Century). The first English translation of the centuries old *Mar Nameh* was by Jivanji Jamshedji Modi in 1893, published by the Anthropological Society of Bombay, India. However, this text has been out of print for over a century and hardly any of Modi's translation remains. It was something of a quest to obtain access to one of the original prints of Modi's 1893 paper, however, I was fortunate to eventually get access in the Bodleian Library, in Oxford University. Modi refers to the *Mar Nameh* as *"the book for taking omens from snakes"*. However, I have chosen to expand the title to include the word 'calendar', as it soon becomes apparent that the poem has implications for the entire Zoroastrian Calendar and view of Time. Furthermore, because of rarity of this text, both academics and mystics are by and large unaware of its existence and its implications.

What follows is my English transliteration of *Mar Nameh* (Chapter 2), followed by a new Persian calligraphy of the Persian text (Chapter 3), and an English translation of it (Chapter 4). The emphasis in my transliteration is upon rhyme and poetry, rather than word for word translation, in order to make this rare text more accessible. This is then followed by my literal translation based on Modi's work.

This calendar and omen system is based on the observation of a snake on each day of the month. Each month begins on Hormozd's (Ohrmazd / Ahura Mazda) day (day 1) and ends in Aniran's day (day 30). The numbering at the beginning of each couplet refers to the day number. It should be noted that the Persian calendar is a solar calendar that begins at the Spring Equinox, which is on or near the 21st of March. Therefore, there is a approximate 21 day difference in the numbering between the Persian and the Gregorian (Western) calendar, for example the 22nd of March in the Gregorian calendar is day 2 in the Persian, 23rd is day 3 etc.

To allow easy use of this system the appendix shows the Gregorian calendar with their equivalent dates in the Persian 'Zoroastrian Religious Era' calendar. The calendars included in the appendix are from the Zoroastrian Religious Era (ZRE) 2006 to 2008. The current year (2005) in the Zoroastrian Religious Era (ZRE) is 3743, this calendar began at the Spring Equinox of 1737 BCE, the time when Zoroaster proclaimed his Divine mission to humankind and heralds the dawn of age of Aries. To use the *Mar Namah*, simply look up the day in the calendar in the appendix when you saw a snake (or dreamt of it) and read across to the equivalent day number (name) in the Zoroastrian calendar, then look up the Zoroastrian day number in chapter 4, the translation of *Mar Namah*.

The ZRE calendar is an attempt to combine all of the Zoroastrian Calendars into one, these calendars are *Shehenshahi, Kadmi,* and *Fasli* which are still in use, for the purpose of the *Mar Nameh,* the Zoroastrian Religious Era (ZRE) calendar is used here. However, if preferred, other forms of the Zoroastrian calendar can also be adapted.

The name of each day here is the name of the spirit, angel, or deity associated with it: Day 1 Hormozd (Ahura Madza the Wise Lord); day 10 Aban (Anahita Sea goddess); day 11 Khorsheed (Sun); day 12 is Mah (Moon); day 13 is Tir (Star Sirius); day 16 Mehr (Mithra) etc. A full description of the meaning for each day is included in Chapter 5. The thirty days and the divine beings associated with them are each prayed to in Yasna 16.3–16.6 (see below). The 'Yasna', which means 'act of worship', are part of the Zoroastrian holy texts.

The meaning of seeing a snake on each day could be indicative of the nature of the relationship of the snake with the spirit of the day. The snake is a symbol of Ahirman (Lord of Darkness), therefore the significance of divination can be seen as the nature of the interaction or relation between the force of Ahirman and the force of spirit presiding over the day. This is the battle in 'time' in the manifested world between Zurvan's (Infinite Time) twin sons Ahriman and Ahura Mada (Lord of Light). In some cases these will have a positive outcome and in some a negative one. Nevertheless, the Zoroastrian texts recommend that its followers should carry with them a 'snake killer' the *maro-gno*, and priests always should. This stick is used to kill snakes; hence followers taking part in the battle against Ahriman carry it. The stick 'snake killer' was also sometimes used in the punishment of a criminal.

The twins are also referred to in Yasna 30.3–4

"Truly there are two primal Spirits, twins renowned to be in conflict. In thought and word, in act they are two: the better and the bad. And those who act well have chosen rightly between these two, not so the evil doers. And when these two spirits first came together they created life and not-life, and how at the end Worst Existence shall be for the wicked, but (the House of) Best purpose for the just man." [3] Mary Boyce: *textual sources for the study of Zoroastrianism* [3].

In the Zoroastrian religion, Ahura Mazda has seven immortal aspects – the Amshaspends or Ameshas Spenta, each of which rules over a particular realm. These are: Vohu Mano (good thought, the realm of animals), Asha Vahishta (righteousness, the realm of fire), Spenta Armaiti (devotion, the realm of earth), Khshathra Vairya (dominion, the realm of sun and heavens), Haurvatat (wholeness, the realm of water), Ameretat (immortality, the realm of plants), and Spenta Mainyu, who is identified with Ahura Mazda (the realm of humanity). There are also seven Yazatas, the protective spirits: Anahita (water / fertility), Atar (fire), Homa (healing plant), Sraosha (obedience / hearer of prayers), Rashnu (judgment), Mithra (truth), Tishtrya (the Dog Star / source of rain).

Zoroastrianism is monotheistic, with a strong dualism, whereby Ahura Mazda's Ameshas Spenta and Yazatas, the forces of light, are faced with the forces of darkness of the Angra Mainyu, or Ahriman. Ahriman – whose symbol is the snake, is called the Great Lie (Farsi *durug*). He and his demons are said to create drought, harsh weather, sickness, disease, poverty, and all forms of suffering. In pre-Zoroastrian Persia, snakes were perceived in a more positive light, indeed Elimite kings, rulers of Elamite civilization in the south-western Iran, wore a snake-shaped crown and painted snakes on their pottery, as seen on a clay pot from 2000 BC. The transition from a positive view to a negative view of snakes could be due to the poisonous nature of some of the more than fifty species of snake in Iran. The transition relates back to early human history, which also might relate to the discovery of fire. For example, the legend of Hushang Shah, who encountered a black snake one day while horse riding. To defend himself Hushang threw a stone at the snake and missed. Instead, the rock hit another large rock and started a spark starting a fire. The fire spread and engulfed the snake saving Hushang's life.

In this system, the first seven days celebrate Ahura Mazda and the Amesha Spentas (the Beneficent Immortals), also referred to as the Archangels. They are said to be the highest spiritual beings created by Ahura Mazda. The second week celebrates light and nature. The third week celebrates moral ethical qualities. The fourth week celebrates spiritual and religious ideas.

The following is the invocation of thirty days' calendar divinities, Yasna 16.

> "3. And we worship the former religions of the world devoted to Righteousness which were instituted at the creation, the holy religions of the Creator Ahura Mazda, the resplendent and glorious. And we worship Vohu Manah (the Good Mind), and Asha Vahishta (who is Righteousness the Best), and Khshathra-vairya, the Kingdom to be desired, and the good and bountiful Armaiti (true piety in the believers), and Haurvatat and Ameretat (our Weal and Immortality).
>
> 4. Yea, we worship the Creator Ahura Mazda and the Fire, Ahura Mazda's son, and the good waters which are Mazda-made and holy, and the resplendent sun of the swift horses, and the moon with the seed of cattle (in his beams); and we worship the star Tishtrya, the lustrous and glorious; and we worship the soul of the Kine of blessed endowment,
>
> (5) and its Creator Ahura Mazda; and we worship Mithra of the wide pastures, and Sraosha (Obedience) the blessed, and Rashnu the most just, and the good, heroic, bountiful Fravashis of the saints, and the Blow-of-victory Ahura-given (as it is). And we worship Raman Hvastra, and the bounteous Wind of blessed gift,
>
> (6) and (its) Creator Ahura Mazda, and the good Mazdayasnian Religion, and the good Blessedness and Arshtat.
> And we worship the heaven and the earth of blessed gift, and the bounteous Mathra, and the stars without beginning (to their course), self-disposing as they are." (From the *Sacred Books of the East*, translated by L. H. Mills [4]).

In addition to each day being sacred to a divine being, each of the twelve months are also sacred to a divine being. These twelve months coincide with twelve days in the month. The conjunction of a month with it's day name was celebrated as a name day feast, hence a feast every month. The modern Persian twelve months (staring on the 21st of March) and their Zodiac names are: *Farvardeen* (Aries), *Ardibehesht* (Taurus), *Khordad* (Gemini), *Tir* (Cancer), *Amordad* (Leo), *Shahrivar* (Virgo), *Mehr* (Libra), *Aban* (Scorpio), *Azar* (Sagittarius), *Dai* (Capricorn), *Bahman* (Aquarius), *Esfand* (Pisces). Therefore, the entire year could be seen as a dance between different Spirits throughout the passing of time.

The months lead into years and during the sixth to the fourth centuries B.C. the Zoroastrians began creating the Great Year or World Year aspect of their calendar. The great year is the time during which all heavenly bodies complete a full cycle of their movement in the heavens. The Zoroastrian world year is 12000 years, and the sequence of legends of 'saviour' and 'anti -saviour' figures has many parallels with the Book of Revelation. To illustrate some of parallels:

1) The theme of the saviour (*Saoshyant*) sent from god.
2) The antichrist (*evil sent from Ahirman*),
3) The whore of Babylon (*Jeh the whore*),
4) The last judgment (*Frashegrid*),
5) The end times (*Khshathra*), and the resurrection of the dead,
6) The fiery horseman to bring the world to end.

It is possible that Zoroastrian legends influenced the Christian book of Revelation. Another interesting parallel is Zarathustra saying: "He who will not eat of my body and drink of my blood, so that he will be made one with me and I with him, the same shall not know salvation ..." [5] which is very similar to Christ's words at the last supper.

The Zoroastrian 12000 years 'world year' consists of four 3000 year sections (see Table 1). The 12000 also reflect 1000 years for each lunar month. During this time these are said to have been three world saviours, each of which were born by a virgin mother from Zarathustra's seeds, that had been deposited in a lake in Persia. The Persian calendar spans several millennia and it both influenced and was influenced by other religious calendars in the Middle East. To facilitate a fuller understanding of Persian calendar and its development, an extensive paper by Dr. S. H. Taqizadeh on the subject is presented in this book.

Table 1. Zoroastrian world year dates, adapted from Prof. Mary Boyce's *textual sources for the study of Zoroastrianism*[6].

0–3000	Ahura Mazda with foreknowledge of the need and means to destroy evil, brought his creation into being in an invisible or spirit state. The Evil Spirit, rising from the deep, perceived this creation. He shaped the lesser evil spirits and attacked Ahura Mazda, and cast him down helpless by reciting the Ahunvar prayer.
3000–6000	The Evil Spirit lay prostrate. Ahura Mazda gave material form to his creation, forming the world in seven stages, with one plant, animal, and man.
6000–8969	The Evil Spirit broke into and polluted the material world, destroying the plant, animal and man. From their seed grew all existing plants, animals and man.
8970	The birth of Zarathushtra.
9000	The beginning of his millennium. He received his revelation, and began to preach.
9012	He converted Kavi Vishtaspa.
9013–9969	A time of goodness followed by slow decline, leading to the present day.
9970	The birth of the first World Saviour, Ukhshyat-ereta (Ushedar).
10000	The beginning of his millennium. He will lead the forces of good and overcome evil. A new time of goodness will again be followed by slow decline.
10970	The birth of second World Saviour, Ukhshyat-nemah (Ushedarmah).
11000	The beginning of his millennium. He will again lead the forces of good and overcome evil. A new time of goodness will again be followed by slow decline.
11943	The birth of the third World Saviour, Astvat-ereta, the true Saoshyant.
11973	He will begin the work of Frasho-kereti (Frashegrid), with the resurrection of the dead, the Last Judgment, and final conquest of evil.
12000	History will end. The Kingdom (Khshathra) of Ahura Mazda will come on earth, and he will reign in bliss for ever.

CHAPTER 2. MAR NAMEH (THE TRANSLITERATION)

1. If thou see'est a snake on Hormozd's day
It wilt increase thine honour, property, and pay.

2. On Bahman's day if thou see a snake in brief
thou shalt meet with some great grief.

3. On Ardibehesht's day a snake in thine haven
Shalt take a relation of thine to heaven.

4. On Shahrivar's day if thou see'est that fiend
To thou wilt return a long lost friend.

5. If thou see'est a snake on Safendarmad's day
Thy dealings with kin wilt bring profitous pay.

6. On the day of Khordad a snake will mean
Thou shalt travel to where thou hast never been
Thine heart wilt be all filled with joy
And thy life no longer strung like a saddened toy.

7. On Merdad's day a snake is cause for worry
Don't look, turn thine head or thou shalt be sorry.

8. If thou see'est a snake on the day of Depadar
All of thy desires wilt be fulfilled in the Bazzar.

9. On Adar's day seeing a snake on the land
means good fortune wilt end in thy hand.

10. On the day of Aban a writhing snake seen
Wilt fulfil desires, for this it means.

11. If thou see'est a snake on the day of Khorsheed
Happiness wilt flow like the music from a reed.

12. If thou see'est a snake on the day of Mah – the Moon
this wilt ruin all thy boons.

13. On the day of Tir if thou see'est a snake
Thou shalt have a place of mortar and brick.

14. If thou see'est a snake on the day of Gosh
A journey awaits thou, further than most.

15. On the day of Depmehr if thou see'est a snake
Thy wishes will be fulfilled by the heavenly lake.

16. On the day of Mehr if thou see'est a snake
Thou wilt soon be rested on a lengthy break.

17. If thou see'est a snake on Sarosh's day
Go home and change thy garment's array.

18. On Rashne's day hit it on its head
With a weapon of stone, or wood, or lead
As sight on this day increases thy defects
Leaving thou helpless with nothing to reflect.

19. If thou see'est a snake on Farvardeen's day
It wilt leave thou happy in joyous play.

20. If thou see'est a snake on Behram's day
Hide thy face and keep all away.

21. If thou see'est a snake on the day of Ram
War and anger shalt be thy dam.

22. If thou see a snake on day of Bad
Thy property wilt be destroyed and be dust clad.

23. If thou see a snake on the day of Depin
Trouble and despair wilt be led in.

24. If thou see'est a snake on the day of Din
Thou shalt be as happy as a harlequin.

25. On the day of Ard if thou see'est a snake
Take this warning, thy heart it wilt break.

26. If thou see'est a snake on Astad's day
Thy happiness wilt not be kept at bay.

27. On the day of Asman if thou see'est a snake
Thy legal world it is sure to shake.

28. If thou see'est a snake on Zamyad's day
Justice and truth will be thine to display.

29. On day of Marespand if thou see'est a snake
To avoid all troubles, its neck thou shalt break.

30. If thou see'est a snake on Aniran's day
Grief and stress wilt come thy way.

CHAPTER 3 PERSIAN TEXT OF MAR NAMEH

مارنامه

اگر مار بینی بروز هورمزد

زیادت شود حرمت و مال و مزد

اگر روز بهمن به بینی تو مار

غمی سخت بینی در آنروزگار

اگر مار بینی باردی بهشت

شود خویش تو یک بسوی بهشت

مشرور اندر به بینی تو مار

ملکی غایبی را بگیری کنار

سفندار مد روز ببینی تو مار
ترا نزد خلقان بود خوب کار
نجز داد گر مار بینی نگر
که ناگاه پیش تو آید سفر

بکام دل خویش گشتن نرود
که نخلین نگردی تو خود با وجود
بمرداد گر مار بینی مبین
که ناگاه پیش تو آید غمین

بد پا در اندر بینی تو مار

برآید مراد تو از هر کنار

اگر روز آذر بینی تو مار

بیا بی سببی خوبی از روزگار

آبان اگر ببینیش در زمان

برآید مراد تو اندر زمان

اگر مار بینی تو در روز خور

به نزدیک شادان شوی یا ز دور

اگر مار بینی تو در روز ماه
ز دیدار او کار گردد تباه
اگر مار بینی در روز تیر
بیابی تو مالی قلیل و کثیر

اگر مار بینی تو در روز گوش
سخن مشنیت آید تو دیری مکوش
اگر مار بینی تو در دی پهر
برآید مرادت ز گردان سپهر

اگر مار بینی تو در روز مهر
سفر پشت آید نزودی نه دیر
اگر مار بینی بروز سروش
بخانه رو و جامه نو بپوش

اگر رشته بینی سرش را بکوب
اگر سنگ باشد وگر خشک چوب
که علت فزاید ز دیدار اوی
بود ناتوانی هم از کار اوی

اگر مار بینی بفرّوردین
فزاید ترا شادی و نازنین
اگر روز بهرام بینی تو مار
از آن روز رخسار خود هور دار

اگر مار بینی تو در روز رام
تو در جنگ و پرخاش مانی مدام
اگر مار بینی تو در روز باد
ز دیدار او مال گردد بیاد

اگر مار بینی تو در در پدین
بود رنج و علّت دلیلیست این
بدین روز گر مار بینی از آن
برآید مرادت شوی شادمان

اگر ار د باشد که بینی همین
که ناگاه گردی ز چیزی غمین
اگر روز استاد بینی تو مار
همه روز و شب شادمانی شمار

اگر مار بینی بروز آسمان
تو بشنوی ز بهتا نهای گران
اگر روز زمیاد بینی تو مار
بیا بی تو داد از جهان کردگار

اگر مار بینی بمار سپند
سرش را جدا کن که رستی ز بند
چون روز انیران بینی تو مار
غم و فکر زان روز چندی شمار

26

CHAPTER 4 MAR NAMEH (THE TRANSLATION)

1. If you see a snake on the day of Hormozd
your honour, property, and and pay will increase.

2. If you see a snake on the day of Bahman
you shall meet with great grief on that day.

3. If you see a snake on the day of Ardibehesht
one of your relations will go to heaven.

4. If you see a snake on the day Shahrivar
you will soon hold a lost friend.

5. If you see a snake on the day of Safendarmad
your dealings with people of world will be happy.

6. If you see a snake on the day of Khordad
you shall make an unexpected journey
you shall return from it with your heart's desire
and sadness will not be present in your life.

7. If you see a snake on the day of Merdad
don't look, as sadness will come to you.

8. If you see a snake on the day of Depadar
All of your desires will be granted from every corner.

9. If you see a snake on the day Adar
you will be granted good fortune from daily life.

10. If you see a snake on the day of Aban
you will receive your desire in an instant.

11. If you see a snake on the day of Khorsheed
happiness will come to you soon.

12. If you see a snake on the day of Mah
seeing him will destroy your work.

13. If you see a snake on the day of Tir
you shalt receive a property large or small.

14. If you see a snake on the day of Gosh
a journey awaits you very soon.

15. If you see a snake on the day of Depmehr
your wishes will be fulfilled by the revolving heavens.

16. If you see a snake on the day of Mehr
you will be on a journey sooner rather than later.

17. If you see a snake on the day of Sarosh
go home and put on new garments.

18. If you see a snake on the day of Rashne
hit it on its head, with stone or dry wood
as seeing one on this day increases your defect
resulting in your helpless from its work.

19. If you see a snake on the day of Farvardeen
happiness and joy will flow to you.

20. If you see a snake on the day of Behram
during that day keep hidden your face and self.

21. If you see a snake on the day of Ram
you will endure a state of war and disagreement.

22. If you see a snake on the day of Bad
From seeing it your assets will blow away.

23. If you see a snake on the day of Depdin
there will be cause for pain, and illness.

24. If thou see a snake on the day of Din
Your intent shall be manifest and you shall be happy.

25. If you see a snake on the day of Ard
Suddenly something shall cause you sadness.

26. If you see a snake on the day of Astad
You can count on happiness for that day and night.

27. If you see a snake on the day of Asman
you shall hear of serious charges against you.

28. If you see a snake on the day of Zamyad
you will receive justice from maker of the World.

29. If you see a snake on day of Marespand
cut its head form its body to avoid difficulties.

30. If you see a snake on the day of Aniran
Count on some grief and depression from that day.

CHAPTER 5. SPIRIT OF THE DAYS AND THEIR MEANING

"One day Zarathustra had fallen asleep under a fig tree, due to the heat, with his arms over his face. And there came an adder that bit him on the neck, so that Zarathustra screamed with pain. When he had taken his arm from his face he looked at the serpent; and then did it recognize the eyes of Zarathustra, wriggled awkwardly, and tried to get away. "Not at all," said Zarathustra, "as yet you have not received my thanks! You have awakened me in time; my journey is yet long." "Thy journey is short," said the adder sadly; "my poison is fatal." Zarathustra smiled. "When did ever a dragon die of a serpent's poison?"– said he. "But take your poison back! You are not rich enough to present it to me." Then the adder fell again on his neck, and licked his wound" – Friedrich Nietzsche: *Thus Spake Zarathustra* [1].

Four days of each month were dedicated to the Creator – Ahura Mazda (Hormozd), the first day of each week. The Creator days are distinguished by the use of 'Dep' before the name of the following day. These four day dedications are suggested by Prof. Boyce to probably be an esoteric acknowledgement of Zurvan, who was worshiped as a quaternary. Zurvan was seen as 'Time' and father to the twins Ahura Mazda and Ahriman.

The first seven days celebrate Ahura Mazda and the Amesha Spentas (the Beneficent Immortals), also referred to as called the Archangels. They are the highest spiritual beings created by Ahura Mazda.

(Table adapted from avesta.org [2] and Mary Boyce's *textual sources for the study of Zoroastrianism* [3].)

1. Hormazd The Lord of Wisdom (Ahura Mazda), Zarathushtra's name for God. Also the name of various kings of the Parthian and Sasanian dynasties.

2. Bahman Good Mind or Purpose (Vohu Mano), presides over animals. The name of the second day of the month and of the 11th month.

3. Ardibehesht	Highest Asha (truth), presides over fire. Asha Vahishta is the Amshaspends presiding over Asha and fire; the name of the third day of the month and of the second month. He holds the key of gate of heaven.
4. Shahrivar	'Desirable Dominion' (Khshathra Vairya), presiding over metals. The name of the fourth day of the month and of the sixth month.
5. Safendarmad	Holy (or Beneficent) Devotion, the Spenta Armaiti who presides over the Earth. The name of the fifth day of the month and of the twelfth month.
6. Khordad	Wholeness (Perfection or Health), Haurvatat who Presides over the waters.
7. Merdad	Immortality or Life, Ameretat who presides over plants.

The second week celebrates light and nature:

8. Depadar	The Creator's day before Adar.
9. Adar	Fire.
10. Aban	Waters, goddess of the seas.
11. Khorsheed	The Sun.
12. Mah	The Moon.
13. Tir	The Star Sirius (Canis Major).
14. Gosh	Sentient Life or the Ox-Soul.

The third week celebrates moral qualities:

15. Depmehr	The day of the Creator before Mithra.
16. Mehr	Mithra, Yazad of the Contract.
17. Sarosh	Yazad of 'Hearkening', i.e. paying attention.
18. Rashne	Yazad of Truth.
19. Farvardeen	The Guardian Angels.
20. Behram	Victory, Triumph over evil.
21. Ram	Peace, Joy.
22. Bad	Wind.

The fourth week celebrates religious ideas:

23. Depdin	The day of the Creator before Din.
24. Din	Religion, also Inner Self or Conscience.
25. Ard	Blessings or Rewards.
26. Astad	Rectitude, Justice.
27. Asman	Sky.
28. Zamyad	Earth.
29. Marespand	Holy Word (Mantra), also specific sections of scripture with certain poetic and spiritual properties.
30. Aniran	Endless Light.

Sirozas:
Prayers and dedications for the thirty days of the month

Sirozas (dedications for the thirty days of the month) adapted from the translation by James Darmesteter, from *Sacred Books of the East* [4]. These prayers reveal even more of the nature of the spirit of each day.

Siroza 1

The first prayer to the thirty days.

1. Hormozd.
To Ahura Mazda, bright and glorious, and to the Amesha-Spentas.

2. Bahman.
To Vohu-Mano; to Peace, whose breath is friendly, and who is a more powerful destroyer than all other creatures; to the heavenly Wisdom, made by Mazda; and to the Wisdom acquired through the ear, made by Mazda.

3. Ardibehesht.
To Asha-Vahishta, the fairest; to the much-desired Airyaman, made by Mazda; to the instrument made by Mazda; and to the good Saoka, with eyes of love, made by Mazda and holy.

4. Shahrivar.
To Khshathra-Vairya; to the metals; to Mercy and Charity.

5. Safendarmad.
To the good Spenta-Armaiti, and to the good Rata, with eyes of love, made by Mazda and holy.

6. Khordad.
To Haurvatat, the master; to the prosperity of the seasons and to the years, the masters of holiness.

7. Merdad.
To Ameretat, the master; to fatness and flocks; to the plenty of corn; and to the powerful Gaokerena, made by Mazda. (At the gah

Hawan): to Mithra, the lord of wide pastures and to Rama Hvastra. (At the gah Rapithwin): to Asha-Vahishta and to Atar, the son of Ahura Mazda. (At the gah Uzerin): to Apam Napat, the tall lord, and to the water made by Mazda. (At the gah Aiwisruthrem): to the Fravashis of the faithful, and to the females that bring forth flocks of males; to the prosperity of the seasons; to the well-shapen and tall-formed Strength, to Verethraghna, made by Ahura, and to the crushing Ascendant. (At the gah Ushahin): to the holy, devout, fiend-smiting Sraosha, who makes the world grow; to Rashnu Razishta, and to Arshtat, who makes the world grow, who makes the world increase.

8. Depadar.
To the Maker Ahura Mazda, bright and glorious, and to the Amesha-Spentas.

9. Adar.
To Atar, the son of Ahura Mazda; to the Glory and to the Weal, made by Mazda; to the Glory of the Aryas, made by Mazda; to the awful Glory of the Kavis, made by Mazda. To Atar, the son of Ahura Mazda; to king Husravah; to the lake of Husravah; to Mount Asnavant, made by Mazda; to Lake Chaechasta, made by Mazda; to the Glory of the Kavis, made by Mazda. To Atar, the son of Ahura Mazda; to Mount Raevant, made by Mazda; to the Glory of the Kavis, made by Mazda. To Atar, the beneficent, the warrior; the God who is a full source of Glory, the God who is a full source of healing. To Atar, the son of Ahura Mazda, with all Atars; to the God Nairyo-Sangha, who dwells in the navel of kings.

10. Aban.
To the good Waters, made by Mazda; to the holy water-spring Ardvi Anahita; to all waters made by Mazda; to all plants made by Mazda.

11. Khorsheed.
To the undying, shining, swift-horsed Sun.

12. Mah.
To the Moon that keeps in it the seed of the Bull; to the only-created bull; to the Bull of many species.

13. Tir.
To Tistrya, the bright and glorious star; to the powerful Satavaesa, made by Mazda, who pushes waters forward; to the stars, made by Mazda, that have in them the seed of the waters, the seed of the earth, the seed of the plants; to the star Vanant, made by Mazda: to those stars that are seven in number, the Haptoiringas, made by Mazda, glorious and healing.

14. Gosh.
To the body of the Cow, to the soul of the Cow, to the powerful Drvaspa, made by Mazda and holy.

15. Depmehr.
To the Maker Ahura Mazda, bright and glorious, and to the Amesha-Spentas.

16. Mehr.
To Mithra, the lord of wide pastures, who has a thousand ears and ten thousand eyes, a God invoked by his own name; to Rama Hvastra.

17. Sarosh.
To the holy, strong Sraosha, who is the incarnate Word, a mighty-speared and lordly God.

18. Rashne.
To Rashnu Razishta; to Arstat, who makes the world grow, who makes the world increase; to the true-spoken speech, that makes the world grow.

19. Farvardeen.
To the awful, overpowering Fravashis of the holy ones.

20. Behram.
To the well-shapen, tall-formed Strength; to Verethraghna, made by Ahura; to the crushing Ascendant.

21. Ram.
To Rama Hvastra; to Vayu, who works highly and is a more powerful destroyer than all other creatures: to that part of thee, O Vayu, that

belongs to Spenta-Mainyu; to the sovereign Sky, to the Boundless Time, to the sovereign Time of the long Period.

22. Bad.
To the bounteous Wind, that blows below, above, before, and behind; to the manly Courage.

23. Depdin.
To the Maker, Ahura Mazda, bright and glorious; to the Amesha-Spentas.

24. Din.
To the most right Chista, made by Mazda and holy; to the good Law of the worshippers of Mazda.

25. Ard.
To Ashi Vanguhi; to the good Chisti; to the good Erethe; to the good Rasastat; to the Weal and Glory, made by Mazda; to Parendi, of the light chariot; to the Glory of the Aryas made by Mazda; to the kingly Glory made by Mazda; to that Glory that cannot be forcibly seized, made by Mazda; to the Glory of Zarathustra, made by Mazda.

26. Astad.
To Arstat, who makes the world grow; to Mount Ushi-darena, made by Mazda, the seat of holy happiness.

27. Asman.
To the high, powerful Heavens; to the bright all-happy, blissful abode of the holy ones.

28. Zamyad.
To the bounteous Earth; to these places, to these fields; to Mount Ushi-darena, made by Mazda, the seat of holy happiness; to all the mountains made by Mazda, that are seats of holy happiness, of full happiness; to the kingly Glory made by Mazda; to that Glory that cannot be forcibly seized, made by Mazda.

29. Marespand.
To the holy, righteousness-performing Mathra Spenta; to the Law opposed to the Daevas, the Law of Zarathushtra; to the long-

traditional teaching; to the good Law of the worshippers of Mazda; to the Devotion to the Mathra Spenta; to the understanding that keeps the Law of the worshippers of Mazda; to the knowledge of the Mathra Spenta; to the heavenly Wisdom made by Mazda; to the Wisdom acquired through the ear and made by Mazda.

30. Anrian.

To the eternal and sovereign luminous space; to the bright Garo-nmana; to the sovereign place of eternal Weal; to the Chinvat-bridge, made by Mazda; to the tall lord Apam Napat and to the water made by Mazda; to Homa, of holy birth; to the pious and good Blessing; to the awful cursing thought of the wise; to all the holy Gods of the heavenly world and of the material one; to the awful, overpowering Fravashis of the faithful, to the Fravashis of the first men of the law, to the Fravashis of the next-of-kin; to every God invoked by his own name.

Siroza 2

The second prayer to the thirty days.

1. Hormozd.
We sacrifice unto the bright and glorious Ahura Mazda; we sacrifice unto the Amesha-Spentas, the all-ruling, the all-beneficent.

2. Bahman.
We sacrifice unto Vohu-Mano, the Amesha-Spenta; we sacrifice unto Peace, whose breath is friendly, and who is a more powerful destroyer than all other creatures. We sacrifice unto the heavenly Wisdom, made by Mazda; we sacrifice unto the Wisdom acquired through the ear, made by Mazda.

3. Ardibehesht.
We sacrifice unto Asha-Vahista, the fairest, the Amesha-Spenta; we sacrifice unto the much-desired Airyaman; we sacrifice unto the instrument made by Mazda; we sacrifice unto the good Saoka, with eyes of love, made by Mazda and holy.

4. Shahrivar.
We sacrifice unto Khshathra-Vairya, the Amesha-Spenta; we sacrifice unto the metals; we sacrifice unto Mercy and Charity.

5. Spafendarmad.
We sacrifice unto the good Spenta Armaiti; we sacrifice unto the good Rata, with eyes of love, made by Mazda and holy.

6. Khordad.
We sacrifice unto Haurvatat, the Amesha-Spenta; we sacrifice unto the prosperity of the seasons. We sacrifice unto the years, the holy and masters of holiness.

7. Merdad.
We sacrifice unto Ameretat, the Amesha-Spenta; we sacrifice unto fatness and flocks; we sacrifice unto the plenty of corn; we sacrifice unto the powerful Gaokerena, made by Mazda. (At the gah Hawan): We sacrifice unto Mithra, the lord of wide pastures; we sacrifice unto

Rama Hvastra. (At the gah Rapithwin): We sacrifice unto Asha-Vahista and unto Atar, the son of Ahura Mazda. (At the gah Uzerin): We sacrifice unto Apam Napat, the swift-horsed, the tall and shining lord, the lord of the females; we sacrifice unto the water made by Mazda and holy. (At the gah Aiwisruthrem): We sacrifice unto the good, powerful, beneficent Fravashis of the holy ones; we sacrifice unto the females that bring forth flocks of males; we sacrifice unto the thrift of the seasons; we sacrifice unto the well-shapen and tall-formed Strength; we sacrifice unto Verethraghna, made by Mazda; we sacrifice unto the crushing Ascendant. (At the gah Ushahin): We sacrifice unto the holy, tall-formed, fiend-smiting Sraosha, who makes the world grow, the holy and master of holiness; we sacrifice unto Rashnu Razishta; we sacrifice unto Arstat, who makes the world grow, who makes the world increase.

8. Depadar.
We sacrifice unto the Maker Ahura Mazda, the bright and glorious; we sacrifice unto the Amesha-Spentas, the all-ruling, the all-beneficent.

9. Adar.
We sacrifice unto Atar, the son of Ahura Mazda; we sacrifice unto the Glory, made by Mazda; we sacrifice unto the Weal, made by Mazda; we sacrifice unto the Glory of the Aryas, made by Mazda; we sacrifice unto the awful Glory of the Kavis, made by Mazda. We sacrifice unto Atar, the son of Ahura Mazda; we sacrifice unto king Husravah; we sacrifice unto the lake of Husravah; we sacrifice unto Mount Asnavant, made by Mazda; we sacrifice unto Lake Chaechasta, made by Mazda; we sacrifice unto the awful Glory of the Kavis, made by Mazda. We sacrifice unto Atar, the son of Ahura Mazda; we sacrifice unto Mount Raevant, made by Mazda; we sacrifice unto the awful Glory of the Kavis, made by Mazda. We sacrifice unto Atar, the son of Ahura Mazda; we sacrifice unto Atar, the beneficent, the warrior. We sacrifice unto that God, who is a full source of glory. We sacrifice unto that God, who is a full source of healing. We sacrifice unto Atar, the son of Ahura Mazda; we sacrifice unto all Fires; we sacrifice unto the God, Nairyo-Sangha, who dwells in the navel of kings.

10. Aban.
We sacrifice unto the good Waters, made by Mazda and holy; we sacrifice unto the holy water-spring Ardvi Anahita; we sacrifice unto all waters, made by Mazda and Holy; we sacrifice unto all plants, made by Mazda and holy.

11. Khorsheed.
We sacrifice unto the bright, undying, shining, swift-horsed Sun.

12. Mah.
We sacrifice unto the Moon that keeps in it the seed of the Bull. We sacrifice unto the Soul and Fravashi of the only-created Bull; we sacrifice unto the Soul and Fravashi of the Bull of many species.

13. Tir.
We sacrifice unto Tistrya, the bright and glorious Star; we sacrifice unto the powerful Satavaesa, made by Mazda, who pushes waters forward; we sacrifice unto all the Stars that have in them the seed of the waters; we sacrifice unto all the Stars that have in them the seed of the earth; we sacrifice unto all the Stars that have in them the seeds of the plants; we sacrifice unto the Star Vanant, made by Mazda; we sacrifice unto those stars that are seven in number, the Haptoiringas, made by Mazda, glorious and healing; in order to oppose the Yatus and Pairikas.

14. Gosh.
We sacrifice unto the soul of the bounteous Cow; we sacrifice unto the powerful Drvaspa, made by Mazda and holy.

15. Depmehr.
We sacrifice unto the Maker Ahura Mazda, the bright and glorious; we sacrifice unto the Amesha-Spentas, the all-ruling, the all-beneficent.

16. Mehr.
We sacrifice unto Mithra, the lord of wide pastures, who has a thousand ears and ten thousand eyes, a God invoked by his own name; we sacrifice unto Rama Hvastra.

17. Sarosh.
We sacrifice unto the holy, tall-formed, fiend-smiting, world-increasing Sraosha, holy and master of holiness.

18. Rashne.
We sacrifice unto Rashnu Razishta; we sacrifice unto Arstat, who makes the world grow, who makes the world increase; we sacrifice unto the true-spoken speech that makes the world grow.

19. Farvardeen.
We sacrifice unto the good, strong, beneficent Fravashis of the holy ones.

20. Behram.
We sacrifice unto the well-shapen, tall-formed Strength; we sacrifice unto Verethraghna, made by Ahura; we sacrifice unto the crushing Ascendant.

21. Ram.
We sacrifice unto Rama Hvastra; we sacrifice unto the holy Vayu; we sacrifice unto Vayu, who works highly and is a more powerful destroyer than all other creatures. Unto that part of thee do we sacrifice, O Vayu, that belongs to Spenta-Mainyu. We sacrifice unto the sovereign Sky; we sacrifice unto the Boundless Time; we sacrifice unto the sovereign Time of the long Period.

22. Bad.
We sacrifice unto the beneficent, bounteous Wind; we sacrifice unto the wind that blows below; we sacrifice unto the wind that blows above; we sacrifice unto the wind that blows before; we sacrifice unto the wind that blows behind. We sacrifice unto the manly Courage.

23. Depdin.
We sacrifice unto the Maker Ahura Mazda, the bright and glorious; we sacrifice unto the Amesha-Spentas.

24. Din.
We sacrifice unto the most right Chista, made by Mazda and holy; we sacrifice unto the good Law of the worshippers of Mazda.

25. Ard.
We sacrifice unto Ashi Vanguhi, the bright high, strong, tall-formed, and merciful; we Sacrifice unto the Glory made by Mazda; we sacrifice unto the Weal made by Mazda. We sacrifice unto Parendi, of the light chariot; we sacrifice unto the Glory of the Aryas, made by Mazda; we sacrifice unto the awful kingly Glory, made by Mazda; we sacrifice unto that awful Glory, that cannot be forcibly seized, made by Mazda; we sacrifice unto the Glory of Zarathushtra, made by Mazda.

26. Astad.
We sacrifice unto Arshtat, who makes the world grow; we sacrifice unto Mount Ushi-darena, made by Mazda, a God of holy happiness.

27. Asman.
We sacrifice unto the shining Heavens; we sacrifice unto the bright, all-happy, blissful abode of the holy ones.

28. Zamyad.
We sacrifice unto the Earth, a beneficent God; we sacrifice unto these places, unto these fields; we sacrifice unto Mount Ushi-darena, made by Mazda, a God of holy happiness; we sacrifice unto all the mountains, that are seats of holy happiness, of full happiness, made by Mazda, the holy and masters of holiness; we sacrifice unto the awful kingly Glory, made by Mazda; we sacrifice unto the awful Glory that cannot be forcibly seized, made by Mazda.

29. Marespand.
We sacrifice unto the Mathra Spenta, of high glory; we sacrifice unto the Law opposed to the Daevas; we sacrifice unto the Law of Zarathushtra; we sacrifice unto the long-traditional teaching; we sacrifice unto the good Law of the worshippers of Mazda: we sacrifice unto the Devotion to the Mathra Spenta; we sacrifice unto the understanding that keeps the Law of the worshippers of Mazda; we sacrifice unto the knowledge of the Mathra Spenta; we sacrifice unto the heavenly Wisdom, made by Mazda; we sacrifice unto the Wisdom acquired through the ear and made by Mazda.

30. Anrian.

We sacrifice unto the eternal and sovereign luminous space; we sacrifice unto the bright Garonmana; we sacrifice unto the sovereign place of eternal Weal; we sacrifice unto the Chinvat-bridge, made by Mazda; we sacrifice unto Apam Napat, the swift-horsed, the high and shining lord, who has many wives; and we sacrifice unto the water, made by Mazda and holy; we sacrifice unto the golden and tall Homa; we sacrifice unto the enlivening Homa, who makes the world grow; we sacrifice unto Homa, who keeps death far away; we sacrifice unto the pious and good Blessing; we sacrifice unto the awful, powerful, cursing thought of the wise, a God; we sacrifice unto all the holy Gods of the heavenly world; we sacrifice unto all the holy Gods of the material world. I praise, I invoke, I meditate upon, and we sacrifice unto the good, strong, beneficent Fravashis of the holy ones.

BIBLIOGRAPHY

Chapter 1
1. *(Trans. J.Gwyn Griffiths,* Plurarch's De Iside et Osiride, *ch 46, pp193–5).* As quoted by Mary Boyce textual sources for the study of Zoroastrianism. The University of Chicago press, 1990, pp. 96–97.
2. The Dawn and Twilight of Zoroastrianism, R.C. Zaehner, New York, (1961), 2003 edition pp 207–208. Also online at: http://www.farvardyn.com/zurvan2.php
3. Mary Boyce textual sources for the study of Zoroastrianism. The University of Chicago press, 1990, p. 35.
4. Translated by L. H. Mills (From *Sacred Books of the East*, American Edition, 1898.) http://www.avesta.org/yasna/y13to27s.htm
5. M.J.Vermaseren, Mithras the secret God, Chatto and Windus, 1963, p104.
6. Mary Boyce *'textual sources for the study of Zoroastrianism',* The University of Chicago press, 1990, p. 21.

Chapter 5
1. http://nietzsche.thefreelibrary.com/Thus-Spake-Zarathustra/21–1
2. http://www.avesta.org/zcal.html
3. Mary Boyce's *textual sources for the study of Zoroastrianism.* The University of Chicago press, 1990, p 19.
4. Translated by James Darmesteter, From *Sacred Books of the East*, American Edition, 1898.
http://www.sacred-texts.com/zor/sbe23/ka2.htm

Further Reading

Tony Allan, Charles Phillips, and Michael Kerrigan, *Wise Lord of the Sky: Persian Myth*. London: Time Life books, 1999.

Mary Boyce *'textual sources for the study of Zoroastrianism'*, The University of Chicago press, 1990.

Mary Boyce *'Zoroastrians their religious beliefs and practices'*, Routledge & Kegan Paul Ltd, 2001.

Peter Clark, *Zoroastrianism: An Introduction to an Ancient Faith* (Sussex: Academic Press, 1998).

Kriwaczek, Paul. *In Search of Zarathustra*. London, Phoenix, 2003.

Mahnaz Moazami, *Evil Animals in the Zoroastrian Religion. History of Religions*, volume 44 (2005), pp. 300–317.

Spiritual oriented poems on snakes is a world wide phenomenon, for example: Francisco X.Alarcon *'Snake poems an Aztec Invocation'*, chronicle books, San Francisco, 1992.

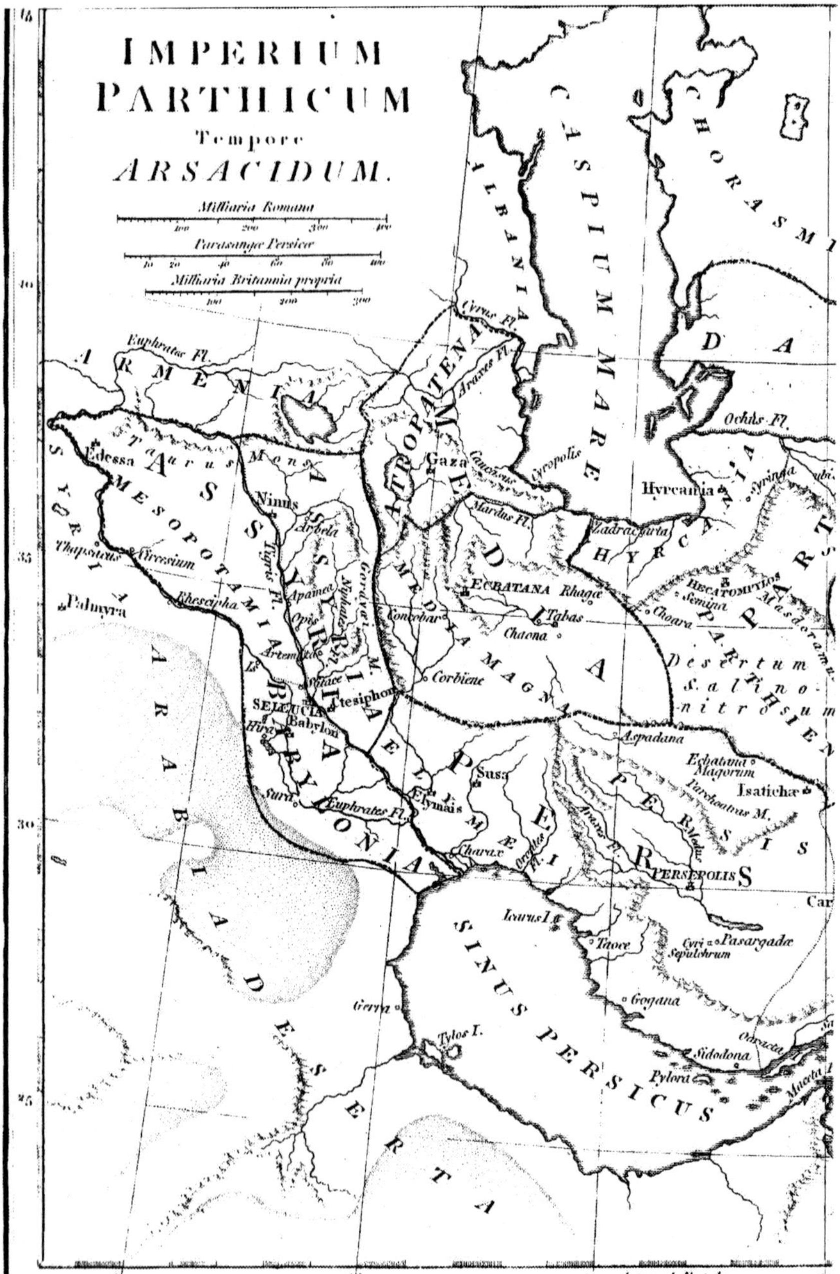
IMPERIUM
PARTHICUM
Tempore
ARSACIDUM.
Milliaria Romana
Parasangæ Persicæ
Milliaria Britannia propria
CASPIUM MARE
CHORASMI
ALBANIA
ARMENIA
ATROPATENA
MEDIA MAGNA
HYRCANIA
PARTHIA
PARTHIENE
DA
ASSYRIA
MESOPOTAMIA
SYRIA
BABYLONIA
ELYMAIS
PERSIS
ARABIA DESERTA
SINUS PERSICUS
Desertum Salsinonitrosum
Euphrates Fl.
Cyrus Fl.
Araxes Fl.
Ochus Fl.
Mardus Fl.
Tigris Fl.
Taurus Mons
Edessa
Ninus
Arbela
Gaza
Cyropolis
Zadracarta
Hyrcania
Thapsacus
Circesium
Palmyra
Apamea
Opis
Artemita
Ctesiphon
SELEUCIA
Babylon
Sura
Concobar
Corbiene
ECBATANA
Rhagæ
Tabas
Chaona
HECATOMPYLOS
Choara
Aspadana
Echatana Magorum
Isatichæ
Susa
Charax
PERSEPOLIS
Icarus I.
Taoce
Cyri Sepulchrum
Pasargadæ
Gogana
Gerra
Tylos I.
Sidodona
Pylora
Oaracta
60
65
70
Long. ab Ins. Fort.
75
40
35
30
25

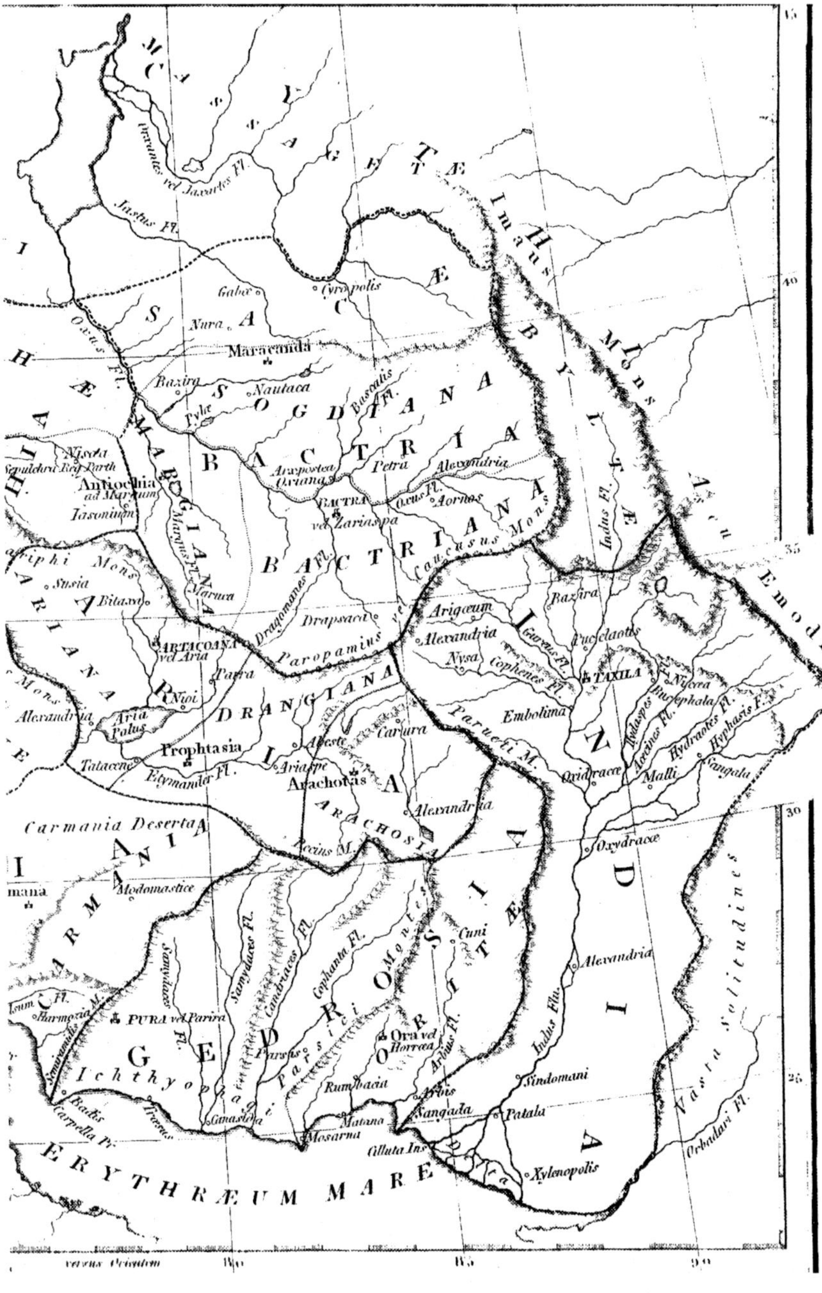

MASSAGETÆ
Jaxartes vel Jaxartes Fl.
Jastus Fl.
Gabæ
Cyropolis
SACÆ
Nura
Maracanda
Oxus Fl.
Baxira
Nautaca
Pylæ
Bascatis Fl.
SOGDIANA
BACTRIA
Imaus Mons
BYLTÆ
Nisæa
Sepulchra Reg. Parth
Antiochia ad Margum
Iasonium
MARGIANA
Margus Fl.
Marura
Araxportea
Oriana
Petra
Alexandria
BACTRA vel Zariaspa
Oxus Fl.
Aornos
Caucasus Mons
BACTRIANA
Indus Fl.
Emodi
Susia
Bitaxa
ARIANA
Dragomanes Fl.
Drapsaca
Paropamisus
ARTACOANA vel Aria
Aria Palus
Alexandria
Arigæum
Alexandria
Nysa
Cophenes Fl.
Bazira
Peucelaotis
TAXILA
Nicæa
Bucephala
Hydaspes Fl.
Acesines Fl.
Hydraotes Fl.
Hyphasis Fl.
Embolima
DRANGIANA
Prophtasia
Tatacene
Etymander Fl.
Ariaspe
Arachotus
Carura
Alexandria
ARACHOSIA
Parueti M.
Oxidracæ
Malli
Sangala
Carmania Deserta
CARMANIA
Modomastice
Bætius M.
Oxydracæ
INDIA
Samydaces Fl.
Cophanta Fl.
Cunaraces Fl.
Cuni
Harmozia
PURA vel Parira
GEDROSIA
ORITÆ
Ora vel Horræa
Arabis Fl.
Alexandria
Indus Flu.
Ichthyophagi
Parsis
Parsici Montes
Rumbacia
Arbis
Sindomani
Sangada
Patala
Badis
Carpella Pr.
Canasida
Mosarna
Mutana
Cilluta Ins.
Xylenopolis
Vasta Solitudines
Orbadari Fl.
ERYTHRÆUM MARE
40
35
30
25
80
85
90

Part 2
THE OLD IRANIAN CALENDARS

The following is the classic paper on the development of Iranian calendar system by Dr. S. H. Taqizadeh, one of the fathers of the modern Persian calendar.

Copyright permission was kindly given by Joseph H. Peterson, and The Royal Asiatic Society.

THE OLD IRANIAN CALENDARS [1]
By: Dr. S. H. Taqizadeh, The Royal Asiatic Society.

[In 1917 I made a study of the history of the Iranian system of time-reckoning, with a view to writing an article on the subject in a Persian review. This took me at that time beyond the scope of the intended article, and the idea was ultimately dropped. I had, however, made a number of notes on that subject. Two years ago I came across these notes which again roused my interest in this question. I decided to carry out the original intention and, instead of throwing away these notes on which a considerable time had been spent, to incorporate them in a monograph on this somewhat complicated question. The work is already in the printer's hands, and will, I hope, be soon at the disposal of Persian scholars. I thought, however, it might be useful to give in English, as concisely as possible, the conclusion reached in the Persian work which amounts to some 350 pages, with some of the principal arguments supporting the opinion expressed therein.]

The Iranian calendar [2], like the calendars of many other nations, had many variations, each belonging to a different historical period or to a different geographical region. The influence of neighboring cultures, the customs of kindred races, or the change of the climate due to the southward and westward movement of the Iranians in their migration from their original home, are among the factors capable of affecting changes in the whole system or in some details of it. We have records of at least six more or less different calendars in Iran, during the Islamic period, besides the well-known Muhammadan and widely used Yazdegerdian systems of time reckoning.[3] The latter, which was, at least down to the eleventh century of the Christian era, the calendar most commonly used in Iran after the Arabian calendar, and which has survived less widely used till the present century, was the same as the official calendar of the Persian empire in the Sasanian period (of course, with the exception of the era). This is hardly questionable, though we have no contemporary report of that period except as to the names of the months. All our information regarding the pre-Islamic calendar is derived from works composed later than the 8th century AD. Nevertheless, we have no reason to doubt the statements of the learned Persians of post-Sasanian times as to the calendar of their not very remote ancestors.

There is also an older reference to the Persian year in a short notice by Quintus Curtius Rufus, a historian of the first century AD and biographer of Alexander the Great, from which it may be inferred that the Persian year in his time did not differ from the Zoroastrian year of later centuries. This author declares that "The Magians used to sing a native song. There followed the Magians 365 young men clothed in purple (crimson) mantles equal in number to the days of the year. For with the Persians too the year is divided into the same number of days." [4]

The Persian year as we know it in the Islamic period was, in fact, a vague year of 365 days, with twelve months each of thirty days, with the exception of the eighth month, which had thirty-five days or, rather, thirty days plus another five supplementary days, or epagomenæ, added to it. The only difference between this year and the year in use in early Sasanian times was in the place of the epagomenæ, as we shall see. Moreover, we know that the Armenians and Cappadocians to the west of Persia, as well as the Sogdians, the Khwarazmians and the Sistanians in the east, were all using calendars which, though the names of the months were in each case different, were, save for the place of the epagomenæ in most of them, exactly the same as the Persian.[5]

Most probably all these six calendars had a common origin. Now we have fortunately Armenian documents showing the dates of some Armenian months and days in the fourth, sixth, and seventh centuries (mostly collected by E. Dulaurier [6]). These dates correspond exactly with the positions which the corresponding Persian days of the vague year would have occupied in the Julian year at that time, according to backward calculation, the only difference being that during a part of the year there would have been a difference of five days owing to the different places of the epagomenæ.[7] A similar inference may be drawn from the Cappadocian dates, with their Julian correspondents, preserved in the writings of St. Epiphanus, the bishop of Constantia or Salamis (Cyprus), and relating to his own time. Here again we find that the Cappadocian dates occupy in the Julian year exactly the same places as the corresponding Persian dates would have occupied if the Persian vague year had been in use in that period (of course, again with five days difference due to the different places of epagomenæ in the year). These dates belong to the years AD 367 and 368, in the first of which Epiphanus became the bishop of the above-mentioned metropolis.[8]

There are still other indirect evidences of the use of the same Persian year in Sasanian times, some of which were discussed in my article in BSOS., vol. ix, 1.[9] Thus I think the existence in Sasanian and even earlier periods, of the same vague year as we find in later centuries in Persia, and which is up to the present day the calendar year of the followers of the Mazdayasnian religion, can be reasonably taken as an established fact. This calendar is the best known among all Iranian systems of time reckoning in ancient or middle ages, and is generally referred to as the Persian, Parsi, Mazdayasnian, Zoroastrian, or Young-Avestan calendar. We shall use this last term in the following pages to designate this particular system as distinct from other Iranian calendars of ancient times, such as Old-Avestan and Old-Persian, both of which will also be discussed here. It is the calendar of historical times and, as stated above, was in general use long before the Arabian conquest of Persia and for several centuries afterward.[10] The later history of this calendar is more or less clear, but its earlier development and the date of its first use in Iran is controversial.

The Y.A. month name found in the Pahlavi parchment of Awraman (No.3), according to the reading of Cowley, Unvala, and Nyberg, shows that the use of these names, and most probably also of the calendar to which these months belong, goes back as far as the first century BC.[11] On the other hand, the existence of two other old Iranian calendars is attested by the Behistun inscription, and proved by deduction from the Avestan texts. Also the use of the Syro-Macedonian calendar in Iran in the Macedonian and Parthian periods is indisputable. The latter might have been in use in official circles and State documents [12] side by side with the Young-Avestan, which may have been the people's calendar, but the two former (Old-Avestan and Old-Persian) must have preceded the Young-Avestan. Therefore the question is often asked and discussed as to when the latter was instituted.

The answer is not easy to give, as the available data are very limited. For more than two centuries many scholars have tried to solve the problem, and have reached different conclusions. Freret,[13] Gibert,[14] Bailly,[15] Drouin,[16] West,[17] and many others have discussed the question, and have suggested dates for its introduction, but their suggestions do not seem to be wholly satisfactory.

Gutschmid,[18] though he has made a profound study of the general subject of the Iranian calendar, was, however, misled on this point (like Gibert before him) by his own misunderstanding of a passage in the book of the Persian astronomer Kushyar (tenth century) as to the coincidence of the sun's entry into Aries with the Persian month Adar in the time of the Sasanian king, Khosraw I (Anosharvan). Thinking that the passage in question meant that the equinox was on the first day of Adar, Gutschmid made this wrong interpretation the basis of his calculation, and came to the conclusion that the Y.A. calendar was introduced in 411 BC. This view found acceptance among later students of the question for some time.[19]

Marquart, however, in the last part of his Untersuchungen zur Geschichte von Eran, p. 210, went a step further in the solution of this problem. He made, indeed, a remarkable contribution towards the solving of different questions relating to the Iranian calendar in the said book, as well as in his paper "Das Nauroz", published in the Modi Memorial Volume in 1930. Nevertheless, his conjecture on the date of the introduction of the Y.A. calendar in Persia does not solve the difficulties involved by the contradictory indications. Adopting West's method of starting from the contemporary Kadimi Parsi New Year's Day, which, taking into account the four-yearly retrogressions of one day, accords with the well-known fact that the Persian year began on 16th June in the year 632, during which Yazdegird III, the last Sasanian king, was enthroned, and making it the basis of the backward calculation, he reached almost the same conclusion as West, with only about twenty years difference. This difference was due to the fact that West had relied on the Persian dates, whereas

Marquart, like Gutschmid, has rightly preferred the Armenian dates [20] because, as a result of an error committed on the occasion of the first intercalation, namely the omission of the five supplementary days in that year, the Persian dates in a great part of the year were five days in advance compared with the Armenian.[21]

Both scholars, however, have taken it for granted that the Persian year at the time of its adoption must have begun on the vernal equinox, in other words that the first day of the month of Farvardeen was at that time the first day of spring. Therefore West has arrived at the years 510–505 and Marquart at 493–486 BC as being the date of the introduction of the Y.A. calendar in Iran. Both authors attribute this important reform to Darius I, who according to them officially established the said calendar in the Persian empire. But it must be stated that the theory of the Persian New Year's Day originally falling on the vernal equinox is not supported by any convincing proof. The idea may have arisen from the impression made on the minds of those acquainted with the Persian calendar by Malikshah's reform in the eleventh century and the resulting celebration of the Nauruz on the vernal equinox, which prevails in Iran down to the present day. The legend of Zoroastrian cosmogony, according to which the "seven planets" including the Sun in Aries,[22] were in their hypsoma or exaltation points at the beginning of the seventh millennium of world cycles, and Zoroaster's intercalation of the year to bring it back again to the same position (i.e. the sun in Aries on New Year's Day), found partly in Pahlavi works and partly in Old-Arabic books, can hardly be advanced as evidence in this connection.

All the above-mentioned hypotheses about the Y.A. calendar have been based on the supposition that the Persian year, even in Sasanian times, was a vague year of exactly 365 days, without any intercalation whatever in the civil year for making good the difference (of about a quarter of a day) between such a year and the tropic year. This presumption is, however, contrary to our oldest reports of the Iranian calendar by early Muslim astronomers. These reports are expressly to the effect that an intercalation of one month in the Persian year every 120 (or 116) years was more or less regularly carried out in pre-Islamic times.[23]

It was apparently the idea of coordinating this tradition with the presupposed adoption of the Egyptian calendar system in Iran in the fifth century that led Cavaignac [24] to advance a totally different theory on this matter. This is based on accepting literally the statements of the Muhammadan astronomers regarding the actual intercalation in the Sasanian period even in the Persian civil year, and at the same time admitting the introduction in Persia of the Egyptian calendar without any change whatsoever (except, of course, for the substitution of Persian names for the months). The prevalent opinion, as it is well-known, is that there were two sorts of year in use: the civil year which was in general use, and the ecclesiastic, used only for religious purposes; that the first was a vague year, and that the intercalation was limited to the religious year. It is also generally believed that, in adopting the Egyptian vague year, the Iranians changed the year's beginning from the season corresponding at that time to the Egyptian New Year (December) to the vernal equinox. Now Cavaignac, though he admits that the Egyptian calendar was introduced in the fifth century BC, is of opinion that originally the Persian month Farvardeen, and not the month Dai, stood for the first Egyptian month, namely Toth. Moreover, according to his theory, though this vague year (without any intercalation) possibly has been since used to a certain extent by the mass of people, nevertheless the Babylonian (or the Old-Persian used in the Behistun inscription) remained the official calendar of Persia until the fall of the Achaemenian empire, after which it was superseded by the Syro-Macedonian calendar, which lasted from Alexander's conquest till the rise of the Sasanian dynasty. He thinks, therefore, that it was in the Sasanian period that the Y.A. or Mazdayasnian calendar became the official and general means of time-reckoning in Persia, and that it was in that epoch that the intercalation in the Y.A. year was instituted, after which the year remained nearly fixed during the Sasanian period with the New Year about the time of the summer solstice. He believes also that the intercalary month was inserted at the first intercalation after Shahrivar, the sixth month (possibly in the fourth century AD) as a second Shahrivar, and that on the next occasion a second Mihr was added to the year and so forth. As a matter of fact, the beginning of the Egyptian year in AD 632 was only ninety days prior to the Persian New Year's Day, the Egyptian being on the 18th March and the Persian on the 16th June, which difference might be easily interpreted as the consequence of three intercalations of one month each, during the Sasanian period (406 years).

Of all the different theories proposed about the date of the introduction of the Egyptian calendar system in Persia, i.e. the creation or the official adoption of the Y.A. calendar, only two are, I think, more or less consistent with many of the known facts and supported, to a certain extent, by tangible arguments. These are those suggested by Marquart and Cavaignac. But each of these two theories has, nevertheless, its weak points and is far from being satisfactorily established or indisputable. They cannot, therefore, be considered as a final solution of this difficult problem.

Cavaignac's thesis agrees, it is true, in every respect with Biruni's statements [25] regarding the old Iranian calendar, namely that the pre-Islamic year of Persia was a stable or fixed year beginning at (or near) the summer solstice and maintained around that point by a 120-yearly intercalation of one month. But besides being incompatible with the contents of the Pahlavi books on this matter and with other evidence in favor of the vague year,[26] this theory cannot be brought into harmony with what we know of the parallelism of the Persian year with the Armenian, the Cappadocian, the Sogdian, and the Khwarazmian years without the assumption of a very unlikely, if not impossible, condition, namely the general application of exactly the same intercalatory system to all the calendars of these different and often politically separate nations. Moreover, it must be pointed out that Biruni himself, who is our principal authority on this subject, is not consistent in this particular point, and his books contain many contradictory passages implying different times for the beginning of the old Iranian year. For instance, his statement regarding the last intercalation, namely that it was the eighth one and that it was executed through the intercalation of a second Aban, i.e. the eighth month (or a second Aban and a second Mihr together), can only be based on the supposition of the original Nauruz (1st day of the month Farvardeen) having been on or about the vernal equinox, and of the latter having been always considered theoretically a New Year's Day.

On the other hand, the theory of West and Marquart of placing the official introduction of the Y.A. calendar in the Persian empire in the middle or the last part of the reign of Darius I, and attributing this reform to that monarch himself, who according to these scholars established the first day of the year on the vernal equinox, is also irreconcilable with the contents of the Afrin gahambar and the Bundahishn on this question.

According to the first of these two Mazdayasnian literary documents the season festival maidyoshahem corresponds to 15 Tir. But the Bundahishn states expressly that from maidyoshahem till maidyarem the night increases, and from maidyarem to maidyoshahem the night decreases and the day increases,[27] though this book interprets maidyoshahem to be the 11th day of Tir (i.e. the first of the five days of that gahambar) probably following its source not very strictly.[28] Marquart is certainly right when he expresses the opinion that the Mazdayasnian traditions are in this respect contradictory and that the different passages of the Bundahishn are not consistent. For while the summer solstice or the time when the night begins to increase in length is put, as we have seen in the above-mentioned passage, on the 11th day of Tir (or, rather, strictly on the 15th), it is declared in another passage of the same book immediately following the former that "in the feast of hamaspathmaidyem that is the epagomenæ at the end of the month Safendarmad the days and nights are equal [in length]". Nevertheless, his conclusion does not seem to be incontestable. He apparently considers the last-mentioned passage of the Bundahishn (relating to the equality in the length of the day and night during the five supplementary days of the year), as well as that part of the former passage implying the identity of maidyoshahem with the summer solstice, as authentic; but he thinks that the gloss placing this gahambar about the middle of Tir, and maidyarem about the middle of the month of Dai, is a wrong interpretation added by the author of the Bundahishn to the original tradition, which was based on the lost parts of the Avesta. Therefore he seems to be of the opinion that maidyoshahem was originally, i.e. at the time of the adoption of the Y.A. calendar, on or about the 1st day of Tir, and maidyarem on or about the beginning of the month of Dai.

Although the original concordance between maidyoshahem and the beginning of the month of Tir in the Old-Avestan calendar (i.e. the calendar of the Avestan people before the adoption of the Egyptian system) is more than possible, the traditional and rather canonical fixing of the places of gahambars in the Mazdayasnian months is, nevertheless, certainly based on the older and authentic sources. These places are given in the part of the Avesta called Afrin

Gahambar. Though it is generally believed that those explanatory passages relating to the places of these season festivals are addenda of later date, interpolated as glosses in the original Avestan text, there is no reason to doubt the antiquity of their contents, which I suppose is as old as the introduction or the official establishment of the Y.A. calendar in Iran.[29] The gahambars are thus fixed at an early date in these places and are stabilized in the months of the religious and fixed (vihêjakîk) year.

Relying on the presupposed principle that the Y.A. year originally (i.e. at the time of its introduction or, rather, its official recognition by the State and "Church" in Persia) began on the vernal equinox, I myself two years ago placed the date of the institution of this calendar in the second decade of the fifth century BC, and have tried to suggest the exact date of this reform.[30] The reasons for this conjecture are given in a paper read before the International Congress of Orientalists held in Rome in 1935 (section iv, sitting of 26th September), as well as more fully in my above-mentioned Persian book entitled Essay on the Iranian Calendar.

A New Conjecture

A later study of the question, however, has led me to change somewhat my former opinion. The conclusion reached is this. The abandonment by the Zoroastrian community of their traditional Old-Avestan calendar, and by the Persian court and Government of the Old-Persian or early Achaemenian calendar, in favor of the Egyptian system took place during the Achaemenian period. This reform may not have been effected in both cases (the "Church" and the State) simultaneously, and most probably one preceded the other by a considerable time. Nevertheless, the final union of the two, i.e. the religious community and the court, in this matter must have been accomplished in the first decade of the second half of the fifth century BC, probably about 441. It was also then, I think, that the beginning of the year was placed near the vernal equinox, and not far from the Babylonian zagmûg (New Year's festival) and that the intercalation system was instituted. The reasons which have led me to this conclusion are as follows:

There is no doubt that the Achaemenian kings used, in the early part of the reign of that dynasty, a calendar based most probably on the Babylonian (perhaps indirectly through the Elamite or Assyrian calendar). Their months were running strictly or almost parallel with the Babylonian months and their year must have been a luni-solar one like that of the Babylonians. The only difference between these two calendars was in the names of the months, and perhaps also in the fact that, while the Babylonian year began near the vernal equinox, the beginning of the Persian year was probably near the autumnal equinox. This last theory, if it should be satisfactorily proved, would suggest that this practice was a survival from that of the early ancestors of this branch of Iranian stock, as the name sared in Avesta and thard in Darius's inscription for the year and their similarity with the Indian sarad (autumnal season) also may suggest. We shall call this Achaemenian or south-western Iranian calendar here Old-Persian.[31]

The people among whom Zoroaster preached his new religion and founded the first Mazdayasnian community (whom we may conveniently call "the Avestan people"), on the other hand, appear to have had a totally different system of time reckoning which, there are strong reasons to believe, was an ancient form of the Iranian calendar of early Aryan (probably north-eastern) origin and of a rural character, beginning with or about the summer solstice. This calendar, which we shall call in the following pages Old-Avestan, has in many respects great similarity with the oldest Indian (Vedic) calendar and in some aspects also with the post-Vedic calendar, and both (the Indian and Avestan) may have had a common origin. The year of the Old-Avestan calendar, which seems to have been called yâr, appears to have been first divided into two main parts, from the summer solstice (maidyoshahem or mid-summer) to the winter solstice (maidyarem or mid-year) and vice versa, exactly like the old Vedic year, which was also originally divided in the same way into two ayanas (uttarâyana and daksinâyana).[32] The further division of the year in later times in India into more and shorter seasons (ritu) up to six in number, which took place there gradually, has also great resemblance to the similar division of the year into six seasons (yâirya ratavô) or gahs among the kindred race of the Iranians, though the Iranian seasons, unlike the Indian, were of unequal length.[33] This later and gradual division of the year in both countries certainly took place as a consequence of the climatic change encountered by Indo-

Aryans and Iranians during their migration southwards, and hence the difference in the way of division.

The Old-Avestan year began, as already stated, with maidyoshahem or the summer solstice, and was presumably of 360 days with two parts, each of 180 days, like the Indian ayanas. The second part began accordingly with maidyarem, near the winter solstice. The very name of this gahambar, which certainly means mid-year with its description or its epithet in the Avesta indicating "the cold bringer" (Visperad 1.2, 2.2), testifies to the year's commencing with summer. Also there is, in Yasht 8.36, perhaps further support in favor of this theory. It is said there that when (or after) "the year [again] comes to the end for men the counsellor princes (? chieftains) and the wild animals, [who] house in the mountains and the shy [animals who] graze (or wander) in the plains, watch [when it (the Tishtrya) is in] rising".[34] The Tishtrya, which is generally held to be Sirius, had its first heliacal rising in July in the first half of the first millennium BC (in north-eastern Iran it rose about 26th–27th July, i.e. four weeks after the solstice). Thus the people might have been waiting and longing impatiently for this rain-bringing star in the first days of the summer. The epithets of the other gahambars, as well as the attributes by which they are qualified in the Avesta, also all agree with these supposed positions of maidyoshahem and maidyarem. Again, the verse of the Vendidad (18.9) which refers to Marshavan, "who could through his wrong religion seduce one to commit the sin of not having devoted (neglecting to devote) himself to the study [of the holy text], continuously for a period comprising three springs (thrizaremaêm)," deserves attention. Could it not be interpreted as suggesting that the spring was the last part of the year, and with the third spring, a period of three full years was completed, which would mean that the year began with summer?

There must have been, in the Old-Avestan calendar, no doubt in practice, some sort of intercalation in order to keep these seasons and the agricultural and religious festivals which were at the end of the seasons more or less in their fixed places in the tropical year. But the means by which this stabilization was achieved is as little known to us as that by which the old Indo-Aryans prevented the old Vedic year from becoming a vague year. If the year (Old-Avestan) was lunar, i.e. a year of 354 days, then the intercalation must have taken place through the addition of an extra month each two or three years.

Apparently this was the opinion of Marquart, who refers to this Old-Avestan year as also "vermutlich ein gebundenes Mondjahr".[35] The analogy with the old Indian Vedic year and Biruni's report of a year of 360 days in the time of Peshdadian dynasty,[36] i.e. in the prehistoric Iranian period, however, make the identification of the Old-Avestan year with this sort of year (i.e. a year of 360 days) more acceptable.[37] We may also accept Biruni's statement as to the method of stabilizing the Old-Avestan year, namely by the intercalation of one month of thirty days every six years [38] [and perhaps sometimes five years], though a supplementary intercalation of another month each 120 years, which he reports also in the same passage about that calendar, seems to be very unlikely in those ancient times. This calendar must have been in use when Zoroaster appeared among the people whom we have called the Avestan people, and it must have remained in use with or without some small changes for a considerable time, thus becoming later the calendar of the early Mazdayasnian community. Therefore it must have existed in south-western Iran in the time of the first Achaemenian rulers as the religious calendar of the Zoroastrians of that region side by side with the Old-Persian calendar, which was the official system for the computation of time for the State as well as for the non-Zoroastrian people of that country.

The first reform
The contact between Persian and Egyptian culture which began with the conquest of Egypt by Cambyses in 525 BC must naturally have attracted the attention of the rising nation to that old and famous civilization. Darius, who had accompanied Cambyses to Egypt and had stayed there for some years before his accession to the Persian throne, returned to that country, after he became king, in 517 BC. He took a very great interest in the Egyptian nation and their culture, treated the Egyptians kindly, became very popular with them, and was recognized by them as one of their law-givers. It is possible he took a good many Persian nobles, sages, and religious leaders with him to Egypt, and be brought with him, or summoned, to Susa the high priest of the famous Sais temple, Uzahor by name (according to an inscription now in the Vatican).[39]

The intercourse between the two nations which developed particularly with the friendly attitude of Persia towards Egypt and the good feeling felt by the latter toward the former, may certainly have had some influence on the institutions of Persia. Therefore it is not unreasonable to assume that it was at or about this period that the high authorities of the Zoroastrian community in Persia adopted the Egyptian system of time reckoning, and thus introduced the Y.A. calendar. The similarity of principle involved by the theoretical beginning of the year in both cases (among the Egyptian and the Zoroastrian community) on or near the heliacal rising of Sirius may have prepared the ground for a *rapprochement* in this matter. The original New Year of Egypt was based on the time of the first heliacal rising of the dog-star (Sirius), called by them Sopdet, which in ancient times nearly coincided with the beginning of the rise of the Nile.[40] This was the greatest festival of the Egyptians, for the rising of the Nile was the principal source of their happiness and prosperity. Similarly the heliacal rising of Tishtrya (generally believed to be the Avestan name for Sirius), which was looked for as the bringer of much needed rain, the most vital necessity for the Persian cultivator during the season of excessive heat, must have been in that country as great a blessing as the rise of the Nile to the Egyptians.[41] Consequently this point of time (or the first day of the month during which this star rose) had most probably been fixed, as has already been stated, as the New Year of the original people of the Avesta in the pre-Zoroastrian and early Zoroastrian periods.[42]

Moreover, the Egyptian system with a year of a fixed number of days (365) without intercalation (for the omitted fraction of day) may have appeared to the minds of the Zoroastrian priests, especially for liturgical purposes much simpler and more convenient than their own. Consequently they adopted that system and introduced the so-called Young-Avestan calendar into the Zoroastrian church and community. This community may have been by this time encouraged, and perhaps even favorably regarded and supported by the court, following the anti-Magi policy of Darius after the slaying of the Magian usurper and general massacre of this caste in 522 BC. Thus the reform consisted in giving up the Old-Avestan calendar and copying exactly the Egyptian vague year in all respects even in the place of the New Year. The Zoroastrian community adopted the same system of twelve months of thirty days each, with a yearly intercalation of five days at the end of the year instead of making up for the deficiency of eleven or five days in their former year, by a three- or six-yearly intercalation. They kept, however, the essential and most important parts of their former calendar, namely the natural and religious season festivals or gahambars and, of course, they replaced the Egyptian month names by the Old-Avestan (pre-Zoroastrian) month names or (in most cases) by the names of their own supreme deity and archangels.[43]

If the Zoroastrian names of some months were already in use, the month of the highest divinity (Ahura Mazda), which was till then the seventh month of the year, i.e. at the beginning of the second half-year, coincided at that time with the first Egyptian month Toth, and both corresponded, roughly, to the first month of winter. Therefore, that month became the first month of the new calendar. If, however, the month names of the Y.A. calendar were introduced at the same time as the calendar itself was adopted, then it was natural that the first month of the new calendar should be named after the same highest divinity dadhvå (modern Dai), the epithet of Ahura Mazda. The order of the Amesha Spentas in the month names which has so far puzzled the scholars may, I think, be explained as follows: Putting the month of the creator on the top (the beginning of the year), the order of the Archangels is followed, not according to their well-known and familiar succession, but according to their range in sitting before the throne of Ohrmazd in the heaven on each side in accordance with their age and sex, as given in the Great Bundahishn. Their sequence is only broken now and then by the months consecrated to the older deities. After the supreme divinity comes first Vohu Manah from the right hand, then Spenta Armaiti from the left, then (interrupted by a non-Angelic month) Asha Vahishta from the right, then the twin Angels Haurvatat and Ameretat from the left (though separated again by a stranger) and then at last Khshathra Vairya from the right.

The Egyptian habit of naming their months and days after different divinities also was not apparently without influence in the denomination of the new Mazdayasnian months and days. The name of the first day of the Egyptian months was identical with the name of the first month, likewise in the Y.A. calendar the first day of every month is named Ohrmazd (Ahurahe Mazdao), which is the name of the supreme God, whose epithet was dadhvå (gen. dathushô), the

61

patron of the first month. Again the consecration of the five supplementary days at the end of the year and perhaps also the 19th day of the first month [44] to the reverence of manes in both calendars (Egyptian and Y.A.) does not seem to be wholly incidental. Now, if we assume the date of this reform as being about 510 BC, we shall obtain the following correspondences: the Egyptian year began at that time on 29th December (Julian) and consequently the beginning of the Iranian year, i.e. the first day of the month Dai, which corresponds to the first day of the Egyptian month Toth, must have been placed also at the same point; the summer solstice fell on the 29th June [45] and the third day of the month Tir, about when the first day of the lunar month in that year (509 BC) also began [46]; the Egyptian epagomenæ as well as the Persian andargâh or Gatha days (five supplementary days of the year) were after the Egyptian month, Mesori (twelfth month), and the parallel Persian month, Adar, respectively, and corresponded to 24th–28th December; the month Tir corresponded to 27th June–26th July, and thus the helical rising of Sirius in Iran could have fallen in this month.[47]

If there is any truth in the tradition reported by Biruni (AB., pp. 233–4) to the effect that, after the coming of Zoroaster and the [later] transfer by the Persian Kings of their residence from Balkh (Bactria) to Fars and Babylon, the Persians paid [special] attention to matters relating to their religion, renewed their astronomical observations, and found that in the third year from the [last] intercalation, the summer solstice preceded the beginning of the year by five days, and that they then gave up the older reckoning and adopted the results of their new computation, the explanation may be as follows: by adopting the Egyptian system, an adjustment in the position of the Iranian months in use up to that time was perhaps carried out. The mere act of making the Iranian year conform with the Egyptian by making the seventh month of the Old-Avestan calendar (the later Dai) parallel (i.e. in full and strict correspondence) with Toth, the first Egyptian month, would have necessarily caused a shift in the places of the other Iranian months. For instance, if the month of Tir, which according to our theory was the first month of the Old-Avestan year, normally ought to have begun on, say, 2nd July, given that the reform had not taken place in that year, it was bound to move a few days back when the first day of Dai was put at the same position as the first day of the Egyptian Toth (about 29th

December), making Tir to correspond to the Egyptian Phamenoth (27th June–26th July).

This hypothesis will also explain the position of the month of Dai which, according to this, was originally in its logical and right place as the month of the supreme God, whereas, in the later order of the months in the Y.A. year, its position (the tenth month) always seemed anomalous. It will account also for the unexpected length of the gah (yâirya) ending with the gahambar of maidyarem (eighty days instead of seventy-five) and the traditional place of this gahambar on the 20th day of Dai (celebrated from 16th to 20th) instead of 15th, which was to be expected as the second pole of the Old-Avestan year opposite to maidyoshahem on 15th Tir.

Both of these points can thus be explained. As it has been stated, the Egyptian epagomenæ being at the end of the year and immediately preceding the month Toth, the Persian andargâh should have taken their place at the end of the month Adar immediately before the month Dai. This would have made the interval between the 1st Tir and the 1st Dai 185 days instead of 180 days, which was according to our assumption the original interval. Consequently the length of the last yâirya (gâh) of the year ending with maidyarem would have increased from seventy-five to eighty days.

In the second and last reform, however, when the Y.A. calendar was officially recognized by the State and was made the civil calendar of the empire, the Gatha days were removed from the end of Adar to the end of Safendarmad, which was fixed at that time as the end of the year. But the length of the yâirya from ayathrem to maidyarem was not readjusted accordingly and still remained in Persian reckoning eighty days in length. Therefore the maidyarem had advanced five days from its usual place in the month of Dai, which must have been at that time on the 15th of that month, to the 20th of the same month where it was then stabilized (in the religious or vihêjakîk year).[48] The Khwarazmians, unlike the Persians, carried out correctly the necessary adjustment due on this account, as appears from the length of the intervals between their gahambars corresponding to the Avestan and Persian ayathrem, maidyarem, and hamaspathmaidyem, i.e. arthamîn, binkhajâchî raid, and maithsokhan raid, respectively. The interval between the two former is (AB., p.237–8) seventy-five days, and between the second and the last, eighty days. This may point to the antiquity of the Khwarazmian calendar compared with that of the Armenians or the Cappadocians, etc. The positions of the Khwarazmian gahambars differ from those of the Persian by five months, and from the original places given in Afrin-Gahambar by three months. This fact may suggest that the Khwarazmians followed the Persians in the matter of intercalation up to the third one (presumably executed about 81 BC), after which the former ceased to intercalate, perhaps in consequence of the weakening of the cultural relations between the two peoples, following the Scythian invasion of Bactria and the adjacent countries about 130 BC.

The Second Reform

The positions of the gahambars in the Y.A. calendar are not easy to explain and have been the subject of much discussion. If the Y.A. year originally (i.e. at the time of its official adoption and the institution of the intercalation system) began with the vernal equinox and the month of Farvardeen, the gahambar of hamaspathmaidyem would have then fallen on the last day (or days) of winter, but then maidyoshahem (or the midsummer festival) with its traditional place on 15th Tir would not have corresponded either with the middle of the well-known summer of three months or with the middle of the bigger summer of six months, i.e. the brighter and warmer half of the year from the vernal to the autumnal equinox.

The explanation proposed by Cama [49] for the apparent lack of harmony in the arrangement of the places of the gahambars in the year, which was considered for some time by most scholars to be satisfactory, is also open to some objection. Cama tried to find the solution to this rather peculiar arrangement by ascribing the institution of the different gahambars to different periods. According to him, in the early times, when the year was divided into two parts only, namely a summer of seven months and a winter of five months, four gahambars, viz. maidyoshahem, ayathrem, maidyarem, and hamaspathmaidyem were created as the feasts of the middle and the end of the said Avestan summer (hama) and winter (zyam or zayana) respectively. But the other two, i.e. maidyozarem and paitishahem were introduced in later times after the well known four seasons of the year, each of about three months, had come in use, thus marking the middle point of the spring and the end of the summer (of three months) respectively. Apparently, Cama also believed that the Mazdayasnian year began originally on the vernal equinox, as his explanation of the places of maidyozarem and paitishahem shows.

That the maidyoshahem originally corresponded, as is implied by the literal meaning of the word, to the middle point of the Zoroastrian summer of seven months is, no doubt, indisputable,[50] though this "Zoroastrian summer" meant only the 210 days interval between hamaspathmaidyem and ayathrem, without implying by any means a stable correspondence between the first of these two gahambars and the day immediately preceding the vernal equinox. It is also true that the gahambars were not all instituted simultaneously. Also it must be admitted that in the later Sasanian times, as well as in the early centuries of Islam, the original position of the vihêjakîk month Farvardeen was considered to correspond to the first month of the spring.[51] But as stated above, this theory of the first day of (vihêjakîk) Farvardeen being on the vernal equinox does not agree with the statement of the author of the Bundahishn regarding the increasing of the night and decreasing of the day from maidyoshahem onwards, or with the epithets given to the gahambars in the Avesta (Visperad, 1.2; 2.2). Maidyoshahem is described there as the time when the mowing of the grass takes place, paitishahem as the time of the harvest of the corn, and ayathrem as the season of driving the cattle home from summer pasturage (i.e. the time of retiring from the field into winter dwellings) and of the mating of the sheep (also Yasna, 1.9, 2.9, 3.11, 4.14). If these gahambars were originally celebrated, as the equinoctial theory of the new year implies, on the 150th, 180th, and 210th days after the vernal equinox, which dates correspond roughly to the 3rd July, 16th September, and 16th October respectively in the Gregorian calendar, the seasons would have been too far advanced in Iran for the agricultural and pastoral occupations attributed to them to have been carried out, as Marquart rightly pointed out in the case of the two latter (Untersuchungen, p. 205). Therefore, we may reasonably hold to the description of maidyoshahem in the Bundahishn as the starting point of the shortening of the days and the lengthening of the nights, and put it on the summer solstice or the middle point of the longer summer (the warmer half of the year). We may also at the same time admit as correct the place given to this gahambar in the Mazdayasnian year in the Avesta, namely 15th Tir (Afrin Gahambar 7–12, Wolff's translation of the Avesta, p 303).[52] This agrees also with the place given to it in the Bundahishn, except that the latter book is less strict when it places the beginning of the shortening of the diurnal arc on the first day of the five festival days (11th Tir) instead of the last (15th), which is the real gahambar day.

Undoubtedly it was these considerations that led Roth [53] to suppose that the beginning of the old Iranian year (1st Farvardeen) was originally on 8th March (Gregorian), and Bartholomae,[54] Geiger,[55] and others have followed him in this supposition.[56] This comes to thirteen days before the vernal equinox. This was the position of the Y.A. year in the third quarter of the fifth century BC. This theory explains satisfactorily many difficult points mentioned above, relating to apparent anomalies, and it agrees with almost all our data on this matter. The only remaining difficulties are in: (1) the passage of the Bundahishn indicating the equality of the length of the day and night at the time of the festival called hamaspathmaidyem, to which reference was made above, and (2) the meaning of the word maidyozarem, which is supposed to be mid-spring. Both these points, if they cannot be otherwise explained, may imply that the year began on the equinox, and could be advanced as evidence in support of that opinion. L. Gray tries to explain this inconsistency in the tradition by supposing that "the year originally began with the vernal equinox, and solsticial festivals were introduced later when the actual beginning of the year had receded by thirteen days (i.e. to 8th March)".[57] But as the gahambars had nothing to do with the civil (Oshmurtîk) year before AD 1006, and as their places were fixed in the vihêjakîk or fixed religious year, they must have been established in the places given in the Afrin Gahambar according to their positions in one particular year, and not according to their individual positions in separate years. For if the place of Maidyozarem had been originally, on the forty-fifth day after the vernal equinox, it would have fallen on 28th Ardibehesht, when the beginning of the civil year had receded thirteen days in the tropic year.

Therefore, all the six gahambars must have been stabilized in their traditional places in the (vihêjakîk) Y.A. year simultaneously when the intercalation was introduced. Consequently these places represent the positions which these season festivals happened to occupy in the civil or the vague year at that date, i.e. they had reached those places on account of the retrogression of the civil year against the tropical year.

These festivals then became fixed, being celebrated always on the same days of the vihêjakîk or religious year, as registered in the Afrin Gahambar, and corresponded thus approximately always with the same astronomical positions in the tropic year but advanced in the civil year.[58]

The statement as to the equality of the day and night on hamaspathmaidyem occurring in the Bundahishn was in all probability due to a misunderstanding caused by the later popular belief in the equinoctial beginning of the original year, an opinion possibly having its origin in Zoroastrian mythology and cosmogony, as already stated, which also, in its turn, may have been influenced by the Babylonian zagmûg.[59] As to the meaning of maidyozarem, even if it could be proved that the word zaremaya means spring, it is by no means certain that it represented strictly the astronomical spring. This is very unlikely, since such a notion (the division of the year into four equal parts as it is at the present day) hardly existed among the Avestan people.[60] It may rather have been a name for the earlier part of the Avestan summer, which was seven months long, from hamaspathmaidyem till ayathrem.

In the long interval between these last-named festivals some other holidays for rest and offering, besides maidyoshahem in the middle, may have been considered necessary. Therefore the forty-fifth day of this interval or the end of the first three units [61] of time reckoning was added to the already existing season festivals, and it was made a holiday of the season of milk, honey, and juice. Thus this gahambar was probably instituted much later than the other gahambars, just as the Indian vasanta (or vasara) was most probably introduced later than the other seasons. This Iranian festival which was celebrated sixty days before the summer solstice and corresponded to 24th April (Gregorian), was called maidyozarem or (roughly) the middle-point of spring in the popular (and not astronomical) sense of the word, i.e. the season of the revivification of nature and vegetation.[62] It is curious that Thuravâhara, the name of the Old-Persian month, corresponding to the second Babylonian month Iyyâr, means also mid-spring, and that in 441 BC, when according to our conjecture the Y.A. calendar was made the official calendar of Persia, the first day of this month coincided with the 15th day of Ardibehesht, which has been stabilized as the vihêjakîk day of maidyozarem in the Mazdayasnian year.[63] It must also be noted that the spring in most

67

parts of Persia is very short and that the weather changes from cold to excessive heat with a short interval between the two.

The truth about the Old-Avestan season festivals is that although they had their fixed places in the tropic year, they had nothing to do with the well-known astronomical four seasons now in general use. None of them is based on one of the four main points of the tropic year (equinoxes and solstices) except maidyoshahem which, as the beginning of the year, corresponded in principle to the summer solstice and was the fundamental point of the year and the basis for the calculation of all other seasons. Maidyarem was not the name for the winter solstice, but since it was the middle point of the year, which is the meaning of its name, and came 180 days after maidyoshahem at the beginning of the second half-year, it fell naturally on (or strictly speaking about) the opposite solstice or the second pole of the year. Then counting backward and forward from maidyoshahem,[64] the point 105 days or seven fortnights before it was made the first day of the Avestan summer, and the day preceding this last point was made a season festival called hamaspathmaidyem as the end of retirement, or the end of the off-season, and the beginning of outdoor or field work, and in the same way the point 105 days after maidyoshahem was considered as the end of the summer (the festival of ayathrem). Thus the Avestan winter began, in the same way, seventy-five days or five fortnights before maidyarem and ended seventy-five days after it. Consequently maidyoshahem became the middle point of the Avestan summer of seven months (mid-summer) which now had three festivals: one at the beginning (or, rather, the day preceding it), one at the end, and one at the middle. The winter, being shorter, was divided in two equal parts forming only two yâiryas (gahs), but the summer, being longer, a further division took place [65] and two more festivals were created, viz. the festival of the harvest (paitishahem), seventy-five days after maidyoshahem, and the festival of high spring or the season of milk, butter, honey, and blooming countryside (maidyozarem), sixty days before it.

Now it is possible that the Zoroastrian community, a considerable time after the adoption of the Egyptian calendar system, noticed a change in the position of their most important festivals. This change was bound to take place as a consequence of neglecting the necessary intercalation that was due on account of the omission, each year, of a quarter of a day by which the real solar year (tropic) exceeds the vague year. They realized then the necessity of some sort of intercalation which, while compensating for the accumulated shortages caused by omitted fractions would not interfere with the order of the days in the months, and would cause no divergence between the intercalated and the vague year in the names of the corresponding days. The addition of a thirteenth month to the year was already known to the Persians from the Babylonian calendar, also most probably from the Old-Persian and the Elamite, as well as perhaps from the Old-Avestan calendars. The intercalation of a month once each 120 years would bring back every day of a vague year to the same Julian day to which it had originally corresponded, though not exactly to its original place in the tropical year. The establishment of such an intercalation, which means the adoption of the vihêjakîk (fixed) year, was probably simultaneous with the transference of the year's commencement from the month Dai to the month Farvardeen. Consequently the established correspondence between the Egyptian and Persian New Year was abandoned, and the Persian year began from that time not far from the Babylonian rêsh shatti and its feast zagmûg. This reform was an important step, and it was possibly connected with some special factors. The successive revolts of Egypt, the killing of the Persian Governor there, followed by a long struggle during the first years of Artaxerxes, and the hatred of the Egyptians for this monarch and his father on the one hand, and the growing intercourse and rapprochement between Persians and Babylonians on the other, are perhaps among the possible factors of the change.[66] Artaxerxes I, whose residence was in Susa, where Nehemia took leave from him in 445 (Nehemia, 1.1), transferred it later (perhaps owing to the destruction of his palace by fire or to his conversion to a new faith) to Babylon, where Nehemia found him again in 433 (Nehemia, 8.6).[67] The court remained in Babylon apparently for the most part until Artaxerxes II moved again to Susa after 395.[68]

But besides this and similar reasons for the reform of the calendar, can we not seek the decisive factor in the conversion of the Achaemenian rulers to the Zoroastrian religion? If this supposition should prove to be correct, then it must have been on this occasion that a compromise was effected by which the Zoroastrian New Year's feast was brought more or less into harmony with the

Babylonian zagmûg, and the Old-Persian feast of Mithra was taken into the Avestan calendar. Thus the court would have given up the Old-Persian and adopted the Mazdayasnian calendar except for the beginning of the year. In this last matter the Zoroastrian priests seem to have made a concession to the desire of the king by fixing the New Year near to the vernal equinox, and more particularly by the incorporation into the Mazdayasnian year, of the feast of Mithra, which appears to have been the greatest festival of the South-Western Iranians and of the Achaemenians, and by officially recognizing it. Also the Zoroastrian composition of some of the older Yashts of which (or at least of parts of which) a non-Zoroastrian or perhaps even pre-Zoroastrian nucleus may have already existed among the Magian communities of Media and Persia as hymns of praise to older Aryan deities or as mythological songs and epics, may have been connected with this epoch-making change. It was then that the incorporation of these materials in the supplemented and enlarged sacred book took place, as well as the adoption of the said ancient and non-Zoroastrian popular divinities such as Mithra, Anahita, Tishtrya, and Verethraghna (who were perhaps the Daevas of the early and pure Zoroastrian faith) into the religion and its revised canon.[69]

The Afrin Gahambar or, at any rate, its supplementary part dealing with the lengths of the gahs and with the days and months of the season festivals represents this period, and the basis of it at least must surely have been composed at this time, i.e. about 441 BC.[70] Although the contents of this Afrin are believed to be derived from the Hadokht Nask of the Avesta, that part of them which concerns the six seasons of the creation and their length, is repeated more fully in the cosmogonical chapters of the Gr. Bundahishn, which no doubt are based on the Damdad Nask of the lost Avesta. Through comparing a tract of the pseudo-Hippocratian Greek work (De hebdomadibus) with the material of the Gr. Bundahishn on microcosm and macrocosm taken from the said Damdad Nask, Albrecht Götze (Zeitschrift für Indologie u. Iranistik, ii, 1923, pp. 60 and 167) has proved that this nask must have been composed not later than the fifth century BC.[71] (Reitzenstein proposes 430 as the lowest limit, Studien, p. 130 n.). Perhaps the absence of Mithra, Anahita, etc., in the inscriptions of early Achaemenian kings, including that of Artaxerxes I belonging to the early part of his reign, and the appearance of these deities in the next inscription of any length (that of Artaxerxes II) can also be explained by this theory,[72] i.e. the conversion of the Achaemenians to Zoroastrianism between the two dates. The absence of the name of Zoroaster from the books of Herodotus (composed about 447 BC) and its mention in Alcibiades, i, of Plato (about 390 BC) may also indicate that the faith of the Iranian prophet had become the State religion during that interval.[73]

Further evidence supporting the same theory

The following considerations may help to make the date suggested as that of the second reform of the calendar more acceptable:

1. Herodotus, who wrote his book in the early years of the second half of the fifth century BC, although he speaks of the Egyptian year and finds it preferable to the more complicated year of the Greeks (ii, 2; Rawlinson's translation, ii, 3), does not mention the Persian year as having the same simplicity as the Egyptian. It may be inferred from this omission, as Marquart has pointed out, that Herodotus did not know the Y.A. calendar of the Persians. Ctesias's mention of the feast of Mithra in Persia, at which even the king could get intoxicated,[74] is, on the other hand, possible evidence of the existence of the new calendar to which the festival he thus names (most probably the well-known Mithrakan or Mithrakana of Strabo) apparently belonged, in the last years of the fifth century BC when he was in Persia.[75]

2. The last of the intercalations (of a month each 120 years) took place, according to Biruni (AB., pp. 33, 45, 118, and 119) in the reign of the Sasanian king Yazdegird I (AD 399–420). This was the seventh intercalation when the seventh month (Mihr) had to be repeated according to the established rule. On this occasion two successive intercalations (the seventh and eighth) were carried out together, one which had already fallen due and the other in anticipation. This double intercalation had to be effected by repeating the months Mihr and Aban in the same year, making it a year of fourteen months. Therefore the epagomenæ were placed at the end of Aban, where they remained till AD 1006, and in some provinces until much later. Now the seventh 120-yearly intercalation must necessarily have been on the 840th year after the institution of the intercalation. As a matter of fact, the 840th year after 441 BC, the date we have assumed for

the establishment of the vihêjakîk year, is AD 399, which is also the first year of Yazdegerd's reign. It is true that Biruni is not consistent in his statements in his different books about the date and number of the last and double intercalation. Apparently he considers this intercalation in his above-mentioned book (AB., pp. 33 and 119) as the eighth and ninth together and he says that all traditions are unanimous in putting it in the reign of Yazdegird I, but it is to be implied from his calculations in the Qânûn-i Mas`ûdî (composed about twenty years later) that this last intercalation was the seventh and eighth together, and he asserts that it was carried out during the reign of Firuz (AD 457–84). Nevertheless, there are reasons for believing that from a chronological point of view, his first report, in so far as the time is concerned (but not the number), is accurate, though his last statement may refer to another small reform possibly effected during the reign of Firuz.[76]

3. The Mazdayasnian tradition, though it ignores the earlier Achaemenian kings before Artaxerxes I (Longimanus), refers many times to the latter monarch (Ardashir diraz-dast) and his successors as good Zoroastrians. According to the Bahman Yasht (II, 16–17), this king "makes the religion current in the whole world".[77] Jackson in his Zoroastrian Studies (p. 168) says that "concerning the later Achaemenian rulers everybody is agreed that Artaxerxes I, II, III and Darius Codomannus were true adherents to the faith of the prophet of ancient Iran". Therefore it is certainly reasonable to presume that the adoption and official recognition of the Mazdayasnian calendar was the work of the first Zoroastrian king of Iran.

4. The feast of Mithra or baga [78] was, no doubt, one of the most popular if not the greatest of all the festivals in ancient Iran, where it was celebrated with the greatest attention. This was originally a pre-Zoroastrian and old Aryan feast consecrated to the sun god, and its place in the Old-Persian calendar was surely in the month belonging to this deity. This month was called Bâgayâdi or Bâgayâdish and almost certainly corresponded to the seventh Babylonian month Tishrîtu, the patron of which was also Shamash, the Babylonian sun god.[79] This month was, as has already been stated, probably the first month of the Old-Persian year, and its more or less fixed place was in the early part of the autumn. The feast was in all probability Old-Persian rather than Old- or Young-Avestan, and it was perhaps

the survival of an earlier Iranian New Year festival dating from some prehistoric phase of the Aryo-Iranian calendar, when the year began at the autumnal equinox. It was connected with the worship of one of the oldest Aryan deities (Baga-Mithra), of whom traces are found as far back as in the fourteenth century BC. The fact that Mithra and similar ancient deities are not mentioned in the Gathas, that they are strangers to the original and pure religion of Zoroaster, that even probably they were considered by this religion as Daevas or demons, and that they were admitted into the Mazdayasnian religion only in later times as lesser divinities of the Iranian pantheon,[80] their hymns having been incorporated into the "recent Avesta", might support this thesis. The month Bâgayâdi was certainly the month in which the feast of Baga usually or often fell. It was on the 10th day of this month in the year 522 BC that (according to the Behistun inscription, i, 55) the Magian usurper Gaumata was killed by Darius and his associates, and his illegitimate rule was overthrown. According to Herodotus, iii, 79–80 (Rawlinson translation, vol. 2, p. 393), this day was celebrated later each year as the feast of Magophonia or the day of slaughter of the Magi, on which day the Magians did not dare to show themselves abroad. He says that "the Persians observe this day with one accord, and keep it more strictly than any other in the whole year. It is then that they hold the great festival, which they call Magophonia", and he asserts that "this day is the greatest holy day that all Persians alike keep" (AD Godley's translation, vol. ii, pp. 103–4). It is very probable that the day chosen by the conspirators for carrying out their plot against the usurper was the same day as the great national feast of Baga worship, when the court was expected to indulge in pleasure and was less on its guard. We may, therefore, conclude that the Magophonia of Herodotus (and Ctesias) and the festival of Baga worship (or Bagayâda according to Marquart's deduction) was in 522 BC on one and the same day, owing to the said coincidence of dates, as Gray is inclined to suppose.[81] But there is no need to assume that the two words were identical, the former (Magophonia) being a misunderstood or misspelt form of the latter (Bagayâda) as Marquart has proposed. As a matter of fact, the tenth day of Bâgayâdi which corresponded to the tenth or eleventh day of the Babylonian Tishrîtu was in 522 BC on or about autumnal equinox. The tenth day of Tishrîtu was in that year the 29th of Julian September,[82] whereas the equinox was on the

30th of the same month.[83] If Gaumata was killed on the eve of the festival, this latter can be supposed then to have been on the 11th of Bâgayâdi, i.e. exactly on the day of the equinox.[84] Therefore it seems to me reasonable to suppose that the great feast of Baga with which the later (Y.A.) mithrakana and the modern Mihragan or mihrjân was certainly identical, was originally the day of the autumnal equinox. This equinox must then necessarily have fallen on the 16th day of the Y.A. month Mihr (the seventh month), at the time of the adoption of that Old-Persian festival in the new Y.A. calendar. This was, as a matter of fact, exactly the case in the years 445–442,[85] when the first of Farvardeen was on 17th March, or ten days before the vernal equinox, and the autumnal equinox on 28th September.

It was most probably about this time that the bagayâda feast of the Old-Persian calendar was taken into the Y.A. year and was renamed Mithrakân. It is very natural to conjecture that this adoption was part of the calendar reform through which the Y.A. calendar replaced the system of the Old-Persian time reckoning. Thus again, the Mazdayasnian month containing the feast of Mithra-baga was named after that deity Mithrahe-Mihr in the Persian calendar, and for the same reason the corresponding Armenian month bore the name of Mehekân, the Cappadocian month that of Mithri and the Khwarazmian month that of Omirê. The Sogdians, however, kept for this month in their parallel calendar a form of the Old-Persian name, calling their seventh month bagakânc (Arabicized faghakân).

Now taking the equinox of autumn as the starting point for the division of the year into four equal parts, as according to Epping [86] the Babylonians used to do, and putting it on 16th Mihr in one of the four years between 445 and 441, the conventional solstice day [87] would fall strictly in the middle of Tir, which is the traditional maidyoshahem, but the real solstice would fall on the 14th or 13th day of the month, i.e. on one of the famous Tiragan feasts, the Greater or the Lesser respectively, which may have been connected in origin with this correspondence. The conventional winter solstice would fall on the 16th or 17th day of the month Dai (the real solstice on 15th Dai), perhaps corresponding to the feast of Gâv-guthil which was also on the first day of the gahambar of maidyarem and paitishahem, the Avestan time of harvest in Iran, would fall on the 14th September (Julian), i.e. a fortnight before the end of the summer. In 441 the above-mentioned correspondence was in some cases perhaps less strict than in the others, but the difference was in each case only one day.[88]

It is a curious fact that many of the feasts connected with, and owing their origin to, the solar seasons and astronomical points of the year, have been transferred to the vague year, being detached from the tropic or fixed solar year, and attached to the civil year. Consequently they have remained in their original places in the latter, free from the effect of intercalation, and have receded against the tropic year about one day each four years. But though they have lost their true and original significance, nevertheless they continued to be celebrated always as marking the points they had originally occupied at the time of the official introduction of the Mazdayasnian calendar.[89] Besides Mihragan, Tiragan, and Gâv-guthil we have in the Persian feast Sada, in both Adar-jashn, in Ajgâr and two or three other Khwarazmian festivals, as well as perhaps in the Sogdian Mâkhîrajs and Amas khwâreh (all described by Biruni), the same phenomena. This means that they are symbolic festivals surviving to mark the original seasonal points of the year, but no longer corresponding to them.

Biruni distinguishes these feasts from the true season-festivals by calling them non-religious and the latter religious feasts.[90] In spite of losing their original significance, the former have kept curiously enough some traces of that character.[91] The Sada even literally has preserved the meaning relating to the original place of that festival, for the word means "the hundredth", and it was so named because of its having been originally on the hundredth day of the Zoroastrian winter which is five months, from the beginning of Aban to the end of Safendarmad. This feast was on the first day of the last third of winter, corresponding originally to 20th January (new style) [92] which is the first day of the second month of the astronomical winter (Aquarius) and the beginning of the severest part of the cold season in Iran. The Pahlavi commentary of the Vendidad (i, 4) expressly says that the month Bahman (of course, the vihêjakîk month) is the season of the severest cold and that it is the heart of the winter. The above facts prove that the Sada, contrary to Biruni's statement (AB. Istanbul complete manuscript), was not instituted by Ardashir, but was rather a feast of much older origin.

It is also interesting to notice that traces of the historical events connected with bagayâda or Magophonia, namely the deliverance of

Persia from the yoke of a detested usurper (Gaumata) by a popular prince (Darius), are preserved (as Marquart has already remarked) in the Iranian tradition in the form of the legend of the blacksmith Kavehi and the noble prince Faridoon (Thraetaona), delivering Iran from the monstrous usurper Azhi-dahaka on the Mihragan day, as is related by Biruni and others.[93] Similarly, in the traditions relating to some of the other famous Iranian festivals, a vague memory of some ancient historical adventures of national importance seems to be preserved. For instance, Tiragan (the 13th day of the month Tir) is, according to the traditions, the day on which the Iranian nation was delivered from the Turanian domination under Afrasiyab (Franrasyan,[94] and Gâv-guthil or the 16th Dai was the day when Eranshahr was freed from the Turks and Faridoon returned the cow of Athfiân (Athwya) to its legitimate owner after dethroning and imprisoning of Bivarasf (Baevaraspa).[95]

It is at the same time also possible, and even probable, that while the feast of Baga or the equinox day in the years after 522 BC did not, of course, regularly fall on the 10th or 11th day of the Old-Persian month Bâgayâdi, and oscillated between 16th of the same month and 16th of the Old-Persian month preceding it (Babylonian Elûl), nevertheless the 10th (or 11th) day of Bâgayâdi was still kept as another popular feast and was celebrated regularly in the old Persian luni-solar calendar (presumably from 522 till 441 BC), now not as a festival in honor of Baga or as the beginning of autumn, but only as the anniversary of the overthrow of Magian rule. Thus both movable and immovable feasts continued to be observed side by side until about 441 BC when the Y.A. took the place of the Old-Persian calendar (the latter ceasing to exist). On this occasion both feasts were transferred to the Mazdayasnian year, and were fixed on the corresponding days of this year. The Baga's feast (or Bagayâda) became the famous Mihragan (the lesser) on the 16th day of Mihr, to which it corresponded in 441, and the Magophonia (or as one can say in modern Persian Maghkushân), the 11th day of Bâgayâdi, which at that time (441) corresponded exactly to the 21st day of Mihr (3rd October), became Râm-rûz [96] or Greater Mihragan. This explains the tradition which makes Râm-rûz the day of the actual capture of Azhi-dahaka [Zohak] by Faridoon, whereas it attributes to Mihragan only the spreading of the first news of the rising of Faridoon against the tyrannical usurper. The feast of Baga probably used to be celebrated for five days, and Herodotus' story of five days continuation of the uproar after the Magi was killed, might be considered as confirmation of this. Since these five days fell incidentally in 441 just on the interval between this feast and Magophonia [97] the two feasts may have been linked together and made into one feast of five days with the first and last days as great festivals. The mention of both feasts by Ctesias [98] separately, however, points to a posterior date for this fusion.[99]

5. The date of the second reform of the Y.A. calendar when the New Year's Day was fixed near the vernal equinox, and the practice of the intercalation of one month each 120 years was instituted, is more likely to have been a year on which the beginning of the corresponding Babylonian year (rêsh-shatti) or the great feast connected with it (Zagmûg-Akitû) fell not far from the same equinox. Out of the years in the first decade of the second half of the fifth century BC, which are more or less suitable in other respects, only the years 441, 446, and 449 agree with this condition. The Babylonian New Year's Day in 441 was only four days after the equinox day (30th March), in 449 it was three days after that point (29th March), and in 446 it coincided exactly with the first day of Spring (26th March). In each of the remaining seven years the interval between the two (Zagmûg and the equinox) was much longer. For example in 443 this interval was twenty-six days. Of the three years suitable in this respect, the year 441 possesses other advantages also, as we have seen. Moreover, in 441 the Babylonian New Year's Day, if it did not fall on the real equinox, corresponded according to their own compilation, to their conventional equinox, which was probably also fixed in the same year on the 30th March.

6. The feast of Mihragan was, in almost all Persian and Arabic literature, always generally considered as the first day of autumn. There are innumerable examples of this, which would take us too far afield to quote here. This is not only the case in the writings of the later part of the eleventh and the earlier part of the twelfth century of the Christian era, when Mihragan had reached again to the first weeks of autumn, but also in much easier and later periods one meets with the word used in the same meaning. This popular meaning given to the word and the feast is, no doubt, reminiscent of its original place.

7. The Frawardigan feast (Pahlavi Fravartîgân) or the feast of manes celebrated in memory of the dead, when according to the

Avesta and the Zoroastrian literature the souls of the pious people (fravashis) visit their former homes, must have been since the composition of Yasht 13 of the Avesta, at least, identical with the gahambar of hamaspathmaidyem near the vernal equinox. The gahambars, though probably only one day originally, were from time immemorial celebrated for five days by the Zoroastrians, the four preceding days being added to the principal feast day, as we find in all Mazdayasnian traditions, but none of them were more than five days. Now if hamaspathmaidyem and Frawardigan were both originally the same as one of the gahambars, as this is implied by the above-mentioned verse of the Avesta, then how is this fact to be reconciled with the assigning of ten days (or strictly ten nights) in the Avesta (Yt. 13.49) for the "flying of the souls all around their villages" and with the traditional practice of the Zoroastrians, who celebrated the feast of manes (Frawardigan, or perhaps more correctly Fordîgân) for ten days not only from the Arab invasion up to the present day, but also in the Sasanian period [100] Biruni tells us that a controversy having arisen among the Zoroastrian, as to which of the two pentades, the last five days of the month preceding the Gatha days or the latter group itself, was the real Frawardigan, they decided to add both fives together and to make the Frawardigan ten days, and thus this feast became, by compromise, longer than it originally was. He states further that the second five, i.e. the Gatha days or Andargâh has superiority over the first. This controversy, if it really took place, could hardly have occurred after the composition of the Farvardeen Yasht, which, as stated above, mentions the ten days of the souls' visit.

The question can be solved without much difficulty if we suppose that the final composition of Yasht 13 was posterior to 441 BC, which supposition, owing to the fact that the reverence of fravashis was in all probability a part of the popular belief admitted later into the religion, rather than of pure Zoroastrianism, seems to be reasonable. We may then assume that the feast of hamaspathmaidyem which was in the last days of Safendarmad or of the Avestan month corresponding to this perhaps later name, was mainly a rural festival placed towards the end of the winter and immediately before the Avestan "summer", and that it was perhaps connected at the same time with some offering, liturgy, or some sort of religious ceremony (possibly also some remembrance of the dead), but that Frawardigan was the name of the five supplementary days of the year introduced on the model of the Egyptian epagomenæ when the Egyptian system was adopted and the Y.A. calendar replaced the Old-Avestan. Accordingly, these epagomenæ called also Andargâh, Gatha days, Panjak veh, Dûzîtak, Turuftak and Panjeh Duzdîda (Arabic al-khamsat al-mustariqat) were originally at the end of the month Adar and immediately before the month Dai, i.e. exactly where the Egyptian supplementary days stood. These days were consecrated, as they were in Egypt, to the reverence of the souls of the departed faithful (fravashis). Later, through the second reform (about 441), the epagomenæ were transferred to their well-known place between the end of Safendarmad and the beginning of Farvardeen, some doubt may have arisen as to the question of the celebration of one of the two consecutive pentads as the Fravashi's feast. To avoid any negligence in religious duties, the religious authorities may have added both together and made the Frawardigan ten days.[101] The divergence of opinion on this matter, however, did not cease, if one is to judge from the different descriptions given in Pahlavi, Arabic, and Persian books.[102] However, the later sources such as the Bundahishn and Biruni's books consider the last five days of the year, i.e. the Gatha days, as the hamaspathmaidyem gahambar and also the real Frawardigan perhaps contrary to their origin but as a natural consequence of the 6th gahambar coming necessarily immediately before Farvardeen.

The Young-Avestan Calendar after the Second Reform

The Zoroastrian vague or civil year continued to be in general use in Persia among the people, from its introduction down to the Islamic period. It was adopted in very ancient times, and perhaps immediately after its official introduction into the Persian empire, by a good many of the neighboring peoples. In Khwarazm its use goes back probably even to still older times, when the year still began with the month Dai, as the above-mentioned order and length of the Khwarazmian gahambars show. The use of the name Faghakân for the Sogdian month corresponding to the Persian month Mihr is also a proof of the antiquity of the use of this calendar by that people. The same is true of the Armenians, whose tenth month is called Marieri, so named according to Marquart after maidyarem, certainly at a time when this gahambar still fell in that month, that is before 321 BC. Their last month is called Hrotic (Frordigân) the famous Frawardigan feast which was originally at the end of this month before the said date.[103] The name of the Persian month Farvardeen may have been adopted later when the feast of the souls stood at the end of this month, i.e. between 321 and 201 BC. The name of the fourth month in some of the above-mentioned calendars (e.g. Tir and not Tishtrya), however, may indicate that their model was the Persian copy of the Avestan month, and hence that they were introduced in those countries after 441 BC. Though the use of Y.A. year declined in Islamic times among the Muhammadan Persians, it did not disappear wholly, and it was still used in some districts in the early years of the present century. The Y.A. calendar to which this year belonged was the official means of time reckoning in the Sasanian period and has continued in use as the religious calendar of the Zoroastrians down to the present day. The only changes which this calendar has undergone are: (1) the removal, in Fars and some other provinces by order of the Bûyid kings (possibly Bahâ'ad-dawleh) in AD 1106, of the Andargâh from the end of the month Aban, where it stood since the last intercalation, to the end of the year, and (2) the omission of the intercalation after the beginning of the fifth century (except for one intercalation, but this was in the civil year) by a limited community, namely the ancestors of the Indian Parsis, most probably in 1131–2 (or 1126).

The Double Intercalation

If on the one hand Biruni's report as to the double intercalation during the reign of Yazdegird I or of Fîrûz, which involves the repetition of Mihr and Aban, in one year, was based on an authentic tradition, and if on the other hand the passage of the Pahlavi commentary of the Vendidad (i, 4) relating to the coldest month of winter [104] really means that the vihêjakîk month Bahman corresponded to the month Shahrivar of the civil year, the reconciliation of these two facts will not be easy.[105] For, as Paruck has remarked,[106] the correspondence between the vihêjakîk month Bahman and the civil month Shahrivar implies the correspondence of the vihêjakîk Farvardeen with the civil Aban, whereas the double intercalation involves the assumption that before that operation the civil month Mihr, and after it the civil month Adar, corresponded with the vihêjakîk month Farvardeen. Therefore, the civil Aban could never have concorded with the latter.

The explanation may be sought in the fact that while the purpose of the intercalation was originally to bring back the 15th day of the vihêjakîk month Tir to the summer solstice (maidyoshahem) and the other gahambars to their original astronomical places, the popular belief in the equinoctial origin of the New Year, according to Mazdayasnian cosmogony, had gained ground by the fourth century of the Christian era and become generally accepted. Therefore, when the seventh cycle of intercalation came to an end in 399, and a new intercalation (the seventh) was due, those responsible for this operation noticed that this intercalation, which ought to have made the first day of the vihêjakîk year (the first day of religious Farvardeen) correspond with the first day of Aban of the civil (Oshmurtîk) year, would not bring it back to the vernal equinox. They found that this correspondence and consequently the right time for the intercalation (if it was to bring the beginning of the ecclesiastical year to the said equinox) was about AD 384. As this time had already passed, and the next occasion, namely about 508, when the first day of Adar would correspond to the equinox, had not yet come, they decided to effect a double intercalation of two months, one for the omitted one of the past and the other in anticipation of the next. Adding two months, i.e. a second Mihr and a second Aban to the (vihêjakîk) year they moved the epagomenæ to the end of the civil Aban, where it has remained. The church, however, apparently still considered for some time the civil Mihr (and not Aban) as corresponding to the vihêjakîk Farvardeen, as this was in fact the real position. After some time, say seventy or eighty years, in the reign of Firuz, it may have been decided to consider the epagomenæ the end of the vihêjakîk year, and the Mobeds may have resolved to adopt this officially. This decision, or the theoretical adjustment, may be the source of the tradition attributing the last intercalation to the reign of Firuz, reported by Biruni in his later book as mentioned above. From a report in the book Az-zîj-al-Hâkimî or the astronomical tables composed (about the end of the tenth and the beginning of the eleventh century) by the famous astronomer Ibn Yûnis (Paris, fonds arabe 2495 fol. 65b–66a), it appears that astronomical observations were undertaken by the Persians some 360 years before the famous observations under the Abbasid Caliph al-Ma'mûn about AD 833. This takes the date of the Persian observations back to about 472 and the reign of Firuz. This may also have had some connection with the above-mentioned reform or adjustment in that reign. If, however, both of Biruni's reports as to the last intercalation, according to one of which it took place in the reign of Yazdegird I, and according to the other in the reign of Firuz, should prove to have been based on old and authentic sources, it seems to me this can only be explained by supposing two kinds of fixed year to have been in use. This means that while the stable year, which was most probably a sidereal year, was kept fixed as strictly as possible by some circles (probably by the Mobeds for religious purposes) it was counted by others (perhaps by the State for financial matters) roughly as 365.25 days, like the Julian year of the Romans. Consequently an intercalation of one month each 120 vague years was necessary to keep this last kind of year fixed, whereas to stabilize the first one (held to be about 365 d. 6 h. 13 m.) the intercalation of one month each 116 (or 115) years would have sufficed. Starting from the year 441 BC the seventh 120th yearly intercalation (which was at the same time a double one) ought to have taken place, as stated above, in AD 399, i.e. the beginning of the reign of Yazdegird, but the seventh 116th (or sometimes 115th) yearly intercalation would have been executed about thirty years earlier, and the eighth one would have been effected about AD 485, i.e. towards the end of the reign of Firuz. The existence of different estimates for the length of the solar year in Persia may be inferred from the different statements of the Bundahishn on this point. This book gives the said length in chapter 5 (Nyberg, Pahlavi Texte ..., p.29) as 365 d. 5 h. and some minutes (or a fraction of the hour).[107] In chapter 25, however, the same book contains the statement that the length of the year or "the revolution of the sun from Aries to the end of the months" was 365 d. 6 h. and some minutes. This last estimation is also given in the Denkard (ibid., pp. 19 and 31). According to Biruni (AB., p. 119) the length of the year was considered by the Persians to be 365 d. 6 h. 13 m. and according to Abû Ma'shar of Balkh (ninth century) quoted by Sajzî (Brit. Mus. MS. Or. 1316, fol. 79) the fraction was held by them to be 6 h. 12 m. 57 s. 36 th. The same is given by Kharaqi (twelfth century) in his book Muntahâ al-idrâk (Berlin Ms.).[108]

It was according to Hamza of Isfahin (tenth century) 6 h. 12 m. 9 s. (AB., p. 52) and according to 'Abd ar-rahmân al-Khâzin (twelfth century) in his Az-zîj al-mu`tabar as-Sanjarî (Vatican Ms. fol. 21) only 6 h. 12 m. This fraction which agrees nearly with the fraction of the sidereal year as calculated by the Babylonians, namely 6 h. 13 m. 43 s. would need the intercalation of one month each 116 years and sometimes 115 years (if the fraction should be taken as 6 h. 13 m.). As a matter of fact, this kind of intercalation (116-yearly) was practiced in ancient Iran according to Kitâb al-awâ`il of 'Askarî quoted by Safadî in his al-wâfi bil-wafayât (JA. 10ième série, tome xvii, 1911, p. 278). The same process is reported also by the author of the Ta'rîkh-i Qum (of which the Arabic original was composed about 984), by al-Kharaqî, and by al-Khâzin in their above-mentioned books, and by Biruni (AB., p. 11).

The suggested existence of two fixed years, however improbable it may be, would explain not only the two different dates of the last intercalation, but also the two different periods of 120 and 116 years for the operation given in the above-mentioned sources. The tradition regarding the stabilization of the year by the government by means of intercalation for keeping a fixed time for "opening the tax collection" may also confirm the existence of a fixed year in the affairs of the State.

Note

The theory proposed above, of the two reforms of the calendar necessarily involves the assumption that on the occasion of the second reform the epagomenæ, though they were put at the end of the month Safendarmad, were not removed in the same year from the end of the month Adar where they had stood up to that time. This means that in that year both months had at their end five supplementary days. It is not incredible to attribute such accuracy, which was also necessary for keeping the strict correspondence existing at that time between the Persian and the Egyptian months and days, to the king's astronomers in Babylon, though the above point was neglected on the occasion of the first intercalation (due in 321 BC).

Conclusion

The history and development of the Iranian calendar may be recapitulated according to the theory laid down in this article as follows:

An original Aryan or the earliest Iranian calendar, belonging to the period when that race was possibly inhabiting the most northerly steppes between the Oxus and the Jaxartes, a land of severe cold, may be inferred from the Avestan verse (Vendidid, 1.2–3) which makes the year consist of a winter of ten months and a summer of two (still rather cold) months. At a later period, probably under the influence of a milder climate in the regions occupied by the same people in their southward movement, the adoption of a new division of the year, into two equal parts from one solstice to the other, similar to the Vedic ayanas, can be deduced from the two old season festivals, marking the beginning and the middle of the year, and the first of them meaning mid-summer. Still later, owing to the change of climate, experienced as a result of the said movement, the summer was made still longer by adding to it the last fifteen days of the astronomical winter as well as the first fortnight of autumn, at the beginning and end respectively. Gradually further divisions of the year were introduced until five seasons were instituted.[109] Thus, the summer of seven months ran from hamaspathmaidyem to, and the winter of five months from, the latter to the former gahambar. This calendar we have called Old-Avestan.

Another calendar of the Babylonian type has also been in use from ancient times among the south-western section of the Iranian race, who, coming in contact with, and under the influence of Elamite and Assyro-Babylonian culture, had apparently adopted some of its institutions. Their year was a luni-solar one, almost exactly corresponding to the Babylonian in every respect, except perhaps in the beginning of the year, which was probably around the autumnal equinox instead of the vernal. This practice of beginning the year with autumn was either brought by this south-western people from their original home, the cradle of the Iranian race, where it may have been in use among some of the oldest representatives of that race or in a certain period of their history, as Marquart is inclined to suppose, or it was introduced in imitation of the system of time-reckoning of some south-western people (Elamites or some of the Sumero-Babylonian cities) whose year also may have begun with autumn.

The Zoroastrian religion which had appeared among the eastern Iranians, whom we may conveniently call the Avestan people, probably in the earlier part of the sixth century BC,[110] gradually spread among other Iranian peoples, and may have had a considerable number of followers in Parsa as well as in the other provinces of Iran. The Old-Avestan calendar became the religious calendar of the followers of Zoroaster everywhere, including the communities in the south and west. With the opening of direct relations between Iran and Egypt after the conquest of the latter country by Cambyses, and particularly after the establishment by Darius of friendship between the two nations, the Zoroastrian community probably changed their somewhat complicated Old-Avestan calendar for the much simpler Egyptian year, which had only a round number of days without fraction, and was not subject to any intercalation. This change must have taken place in the later part of the sixth century BC.

The strict copying of the Egyptian calendar, except in the month names and religious festivals, involved the fixing of the beginning of the year in the month Dai, which was at that time about the winter solstice. The year, now becoming vague began to move backward in the tropical year, and consequently the places of religious season festivals (gahambars) were changing in each year. This instability, which was certainly noticed after some years, say half a century, became striking, and was very inconvenient for the Mobeds. The priests then found it necessary to prevent this variation in the positions of the holidays by inventing a fixed year for religious purposes, and especially for keeping the gahambars in their seasonal places. This sort of year, called vihêjakîk, which was in actual use in religious circles and was by no means a wholly fictitious year, as some seem to believe, was created through the institution of an intercalation of one full month in each cycle of 120 (or 116) years. It is reasonable to assume that this reform, together with the alteration in the date of the beginning of the year from the Egyptian New Year's Day to approximately the Babylonian new year, (i.e. around the vernal equinox), may have taken place simultaneously with the conversion of the Achaemenian kings to the Zoroastrian faith. The traditional places of the gahambar in the year which are, no doubt, the positions these festivals held at the time of their stabilization, point to the date of this reform being about 441 BC.[111]

Notes:
1. This paper was composed in November, 1937.
2. The abbreviations used in this article are: B.= Biruni, AB. = al-Âthâr al-bâqiya (Sachau's edition), M.= Maquart, Y.A.= Young-Avestan, ga.= gahambar, gas.= gahambars.
3. I propose to deal with these calendars later.
4. Curtius, iii, 3, 10.
5. The Sistanian year even in this respect, i.e. the place of the supplementary days, had no difference from the Persian year, but in the other four calendars these days were invariably at the end of the year. The Persian epagomenæ were, as is known, moved a month forward every 120 years.
6. Recherches sur la chronologie armenienne, technique et historique, Paris, 1859.
7. It would take us too far afield to dwell upon the details of these Armenian dates here. It will suffice to say that Agathangelos, the Armenian historian of the fourth century, gives according to M. (Das Nauroz) the beginning of the Armenian year in 304 as corresponding to 11th September. The Persian New Year on that date was no doubt on the 6th September.
8. Though the Cappadocian year has been officially stabilized by the introduction of the Julian system of intercalation, apparently about 63 BC, following the establishment of the Roman rule in that country in the same year, the old vague year has, nevertheless, survived a long time after that date and has continued to be the popular means of time reckoning of the common people.
9. "Some chronological data relating to the Sasanian period."
10. Some small changes, however, have taken place from time to time during the Islamic period, and these must be described in an article dealing with the calendars of that period.
11. The document in question was written twelve years before the Christian era.
12. It was certainly used on Parthian coins with Greek letters. According to Drouin (Revue Archéologique, Juillet-Decembre, 1889) even the Macedonian months appear on the tetradrachms from the time of Phraates IV (37–4 BC) down to AD 190.
13. "De l'ancienne année des Perses," 1742, published in l'Histoire de l'Académie Royale des inscriptions et belles lettres, tome 16, Paris, 1751, partie, 2, les memoires.

14. "Nouvelles observations sur l'annee des anciens Perses," in l'Histoire de l'Académie Royale des inscriptions, etc., tome 31, Paris, 1788, Mémoires pp. 51–80.
15. Traité de l'Astronomie indienne et orientale, Paris, 1787.
16. Revue Archéologique, 1888–9.
17. SBE, 47, introd., pp. 42–7.
18. Über des iranishe Jahr in Berichte über die Verhandlungen der königlichen sächsischen Gesellschaft der Wissenschaften, 1862.
19. For instance, Spiegel has accepted it in his Eranische Alterthumskunde, iii, 670, and even M. in the first part of his Untersuchungen, p. 64, has followed that famous scholar.
20. West also has made his backward calculation by taking back the new year's day 0.2422 day for each year from its present place, which is not strictly accurate for ancient times. M. apparently took the Julian days as his basis.
21. The first day of the Armenian year during which the accession of Yazdegird took place corresponded to 21st June, 632.
22. According to one version the sun was on the first point of Aries at midday of the day Ohrmazd of the month of Farvardeen.
23. Only the Pahlavi book Denkard speaks of a double system and two sorts of years.
24. JA, t. 202, 1923, pp. 106–110.
25. There are, of course, also similar statements by older, though less famous, writers.
26. Such as the changing positions of gahambars, the distribution of the months among the four seasons in Bundahishn beginning with the spring, maidyoshahem being the season of cutting the grass according to Visperad, and its place in the middle of the month Tir according to Afrin gahambar, and the two apparently different but really identical dates for Zoroaster's death in Zadspram, as well as the correspondence apparently given to the month Bahman and Shahrivar in the Pahlavi commentary of Vendidad (i, 4), and some other data discussed by the present writer in BSOS. ix, 1.
27. Bundahishn, West's translation, xxv, 2–3. Justis p. 34.
28. The real gahambar day in each of the season festivals of five days duration is most probably the last or the fifth day. But apparently the author of the Bundahishn, notwithstanding the fact that the point of time after which the day decreases and the night increases can only be one day, has considered all the five days of maidyoshahem roughly as

the longest days of the year and equal in length. He has perhaps believed these days to be a stationary period, just as he considers the day and night equal in length in all the last five days of the year (in the same chapter). The whole passage relating to the two festivals of solstices, must be a faithful quotation from a very much older source (possibly the lost parts of the Avesta) without any interpolation except for the identification of maidyoshahem with 11th Tir.

29. This part of Afrin gahambar 3, 9–12, dealing with the length of the six seasons and the places of the festivals in the months is, according to Hertel (Die awestischen Jahrenszeitenfeste, Afrinagan, 3, p. 22), found only in seven out of thirty-one manuscripts of Avesta. Nevertheless, Hertel thinks this is taken from the Hadokht Nask of the Avesta.

30. I have proposed the 28th March, 487 BC, for the epoch of this reform.

31. The idea of the Old-Persian year having been borrowed from a neighboring people of the West (possibly Elamites), who in their turn might have adopted in much older times the calendar system of one of the Sumero-Babylonian cities which had the autumnal New Year, could also be considered if this last theory about those cities could be proved. Indeed, Hommel (ERE-calendar) asserts that in the oldest forms of the so-called Chaldean calendars, e.g. those used in Ur, Girso, etc., the beginning of the year was in autumn. S. A. Pallis also (The Babylonian akîtû Festival, p.30) states that "in the time of Sargon of Agade, Gudea, and partly also in the time of Hammurabi, the New Year began in Tishritu, and not until after that time in Nisan". He states further (pp. 30–31) that under Hammurabi perhaps the beginning of the civil year was transferred from Tishritu to Nisan, but that "in astronomical calculation, however, the autumnal equinox was still used as the point of departure". But Father Schaumberger, who is a great authority on questions relating to the Assyro-Babylonian astronomy and calendar, informs me in reply to my inquiry that there is only one passage (K 775 = Thompson, Reports of the Magicians and Astrologers of Nineveh and Babylon, 16, 5s.) where two different dates (Nisan and Tishri), i.e. the spring and the autumn, are mentioned as the beginning of the year similar to the Jewish calendar, but that we have no proof for assuming that the Babylonians used in their real life an autumnal New Year. This venerable scholar contests also the actual use of a year of 360 days in

Babylon or Sumer (also advanced by Hommel), and says that we have no proof for it though there are some texts speaking of months of thirty days or of a year of 6 x 60 days, which could be explained by the fact that in Babylonian business documents the months are counted as thirty days.

32. According to Kaye (Hindu Astronomy, Memoirs of the Archaeological Survey of India, No.18, p.27), there is in the Rig-Veda also a division of the year from one equinox to the other called Devayana and Pitryana, but the basis of the Vedic calendar seems to be the two solstitial divisions.

33. The Indian seasons are each of two months and all are equal in length.

34. I have followed more or less strictly F. Wolff's translation, with which most scholars agree, but Lommel in his Die Yäsht's des Awesta, p. 54, gives the translation of the words in italics above as "the annual tilling" (Jahresbestellung). If that part of the Avestan word connected with the word "year" should not prove to mean the "end" then the whole argument loses its basis.

35. Untersuchungen, p. 206.

36. AB., p. 11.

37. The year of 360 days was perhaps the first step in the transition from a lunar to a solar year, being half-way between 354 and 365 days. Some scholars believe that this sort of year existed also in Babylon and Nippur (see note 1, p. 13 supra), and there are others who suppose that the vague year of 365 days was preceded also in Egypt in prehistoric times by the same system, though there is no unanimity on this point.

38. This sort of intercalation may be a very old Aryan or Indo-European practice. Could not the six yearly feast of the calendar of the Hittites, which Goetze translates as Sechsjahresfest (Kulturgeschichte des alten Orient, Kleinasien, p. 154), be also a feast of intercalation? If this form of intercalation was really in use, then there would have been no real divergence between the dates of the Old-Avestan years with the Y.A. In this case the Zoroastrians would not have found it difficult at all to change their system to that of the Egyptians, as no real change in the position of days and months was involved. This may also give a clue to the approximate date of the institution of the Old-Avestan calendar or of the said system of intercalation which will be referred to later.

39. Cf. E. Meyer, article "Darius" in Encyclopedia Britannica, 14th edition.

40. Sirius' heliacal rising for Memphis was according to the latest calculation (Neugebauer's Hilfstafeln) from 3160 to 2640 BC on the 17th July, from 1420 to 1050 on the 18th, and from 230 BC to AD 20 on the 19th July, varying between two consecutive days during the intervals. The Nile's rising in Egypt began, according to Ginzel (Handbuch der Chronologie, i, p. 190), in the twenty-eighth century BC, on 16th July. The Egyptian calendar with its vague year, as we know it, is supposed, according to the latest conjecture, to have been adopted in the same century when Sirius' heliacal rising fell on the 1st Toth. This was the 17th July, 2768 BC, i.e. the day after the beginning of the rise of the Nile.

41. The custom of sprinkling water on each other on the day of the Tiragan feast (13th day of the month of Tir-Tishtryehe), practiced down to much later ages, may have been a survival of its original significance, i.e. the anticipation of the coming rain of which the appearance of Sirius on the horizon at dawn was a good tiding. In the later story of the genesis of the world the creation of the water was put on the division (gah) of the year ending with maidyoshahem, which was on 15 Tir.

42. It is probable that the month of Tir, which we have assumed to have been the first month of the Old-Avestan year, originally began in the last days of (Julian) July, at about the time of the heliacal rising of Sirius in Northern Iran, and gradually receded until it fell, in the last part of the sixth century, three or four weeks earlier (i.e. it originally corresponded roughly to 28th July–26th August and in 510 BC to 2nd–31st July). The verses 13, 16, and 18 of Yasht 8, which tell of three consecutive ten-day periods, during which Tishtrya, after its rising, fights against Apaosha, the demon of drought, may refer to the three decades of the month, as Lommel remarks, (Die Yäsht's des Awesta, p.47) and may confirm the correspondence of the heliacal rising of Tishtrya with the first day of the month of the same name. As a matter of fact, the decrease of the heat and the beginning of the rain is quite natural thirty-three days after the heliacal rising of Sirius in the northern regions of Iran. This would correspond to about 22nd August (Gregorian). The retrocession of the month Tir against the tropic year may have been due either to the deficiency of the unknown system of intercalation used in the Old-Avestan calendar,

or may have been caused by the abandonment of the sidereal year in time reckoning. The retrocession may have been slow or fast, according to the extent of the difference of the year with the real solar year (tropical). Having no information as to the rate of this retrocession, we cannot discover the date of the original correspondence between the first day of Tir and the heliacal rising of Sirius, which was probably also not far from the date of the original composition of the oldest part of the non-Zoroastrian nucleus of that older Yasht (Tishtrya Yasht). With a year of 300 days and the intercalation of a month each six years this would take about a century or a little more, and if this kind of calendar really preceded the Y.A., its institution (or, at least, the original composition of that part of the said Yasht) can be reasonably put in the second half of the seventh century BC. As the full visibility of Sirius in the Eastern horizon at dawn by everybody may be sometimes later than the date of its first heliacal rising, according to the astronomical calculation (see Ginzel, iii, p. 368), this would put the date of the first rain still later towards the end of summer and hence more in keeping with actual conditions in Northern Iran.

43. As to the question whether the months with the names of Tishryehe, Mithrahe, and Apam(napâtô) existed in the Old-Avestan calendar, and were not changed in spite of these names being unpopular with the early followers of Zoroaster, or they were received into the Y.A. calendar on the occasion of the second reform (see infra), there is no tangible evidence in favor of one or the other theory. In the second case the introduction of these, names must have followed the admittance of these non-Zoroastrian deities into the Mazdayasnian pantheon. It is possible that the months with these names belonged to the older and popular calendar of Iranian peoples other than the Avestan, especially the Western Magian community, who went over later to Zoroaster's faith. The form of the name of the fourth month (Tir) in the calendar of all the peoples using the Y.A. year may be supposed to point to its Old-Persian origin and to suggest that it was received into the Y.A. calendar in the Persian period.

44. The 19th day of the month Farvardeen (the first month of the year in later periods) is called Frawardigan, i.e. by the same name as the five supplementary or Gatha days. It is possible that in the first period the 19th day of the month Dai (then the first month of the

91

year) bore this name and was consecrated to the same duties as the 19th Farvardeen in later times. The possibility of the transmission of the name from one to the other on some occasion of the eventual concordance between the two is, from a practical point of view, very remote.

45. More strictly at about 2:30 a.m. of that day in Iran.

46. The new moon was in Iran on 26th June about 6–7 o'clock p.m., thus the day following the first visibility of the crescent was, most probably, the 29th June.

47. According to Nöther's calculation (Geiger, Ostiranische Kultur, p. 309) in the regions with 38 ° of latitude, Sirius must have risen in the middle of the seventh century BC on the 1st day of August at 3.3 a.m. Accordingly the time of its rising on 26th July at the end of sixth century BC will be approximately 3:20 a.m. and on the 1st July about 5:10. Thus the first appearance of this star at dawn could have taken place in the last part of Tir. Had the Y.A. year originally, i.e. at the time of its introduction in Persia, began with the first day of Farvardeen and the vernal equinox, as some prefer to believe, the month Tir would have corresponded to 26th June–24th July, which brings it to a still earlier date and makes the heliacal rising of Sirius in this month more questionable.

48. In most cases throughout these pages it is the last of the five days of each season festival which is meant by the gahambars, as this is generally believed to be the real or the main day of the feast.

49. K. R. Cama, Actes du VI Congrès International des Orientalistes, 3, 583–92.

50. J. Hertel, however, believes that the positions of maidyoshahem and maidyarem were in early times the reverse of their later positions and that through a later reform they interchanged their places in the year (see his work Die awestische Jahreszeitenfeste).

51. Bundahishn gives Farvardeen, Ardibehesht, and Hordad as the three months of the spring (Justi's translation, p. 35), but this and similar records point only to the conception prevalent in later times, originating in the post-Sasanian period. I think all these possibly go back to a reform carried out in the time of Sasanian King Firuz (457–84), to which reference, will he made in the following pages.

52. As it is said this part of Afrin, which in some manuscripts gives the dates of the days and months of the gahambars or season-festivals in the vihêjakîk year and months, is believed to be a later

addition. Nevertheless, its original source at least must have been composed not later than the date of the first intercalation (presumably in the last quarter of the fourth century BC), if not as early as the time of the institution of the intercalary system and the stabilization of the vihêjakîk year in the middle of the fifth century.
53. ZDMG, 34, p.701.
54. Altiranishes Wörterbuch, pp. 160, 838, 1117, 1118, 1776.
55. Op. cit., p. 322, where he puts it on 9th March.
56. They did not say, however, what they meant by "original position" end have not proposed a date for this original year, though this naturally implies a certain point of time after which the year should have become vague and altering its position with respect to the tropic year.
57. Jackson, Zoroastrian Studies, pp. 128–9.
58. The gahambars under the influence of intercalation, fell one month later in the civil year, after each intercalation. With the last intercalation they reached to points eight months posterior to their original places: e.g. maidyoshahem corresponded then to the 15th day of the month of Safendarmad of the civil year as B. and others give it.
59. This belief may have its origin in, or have become general as the result of, a reform at the time of Firuz, which will he discussed in this article.
60. The word vanhar, which is perhaps from the same root as the Indian vasar, must have also been used for spring, not in its strictly technical meaning, beginning with the vernal equinox and ending with the summer solstice, but, as in common parlance, for the period of verdure and blossom.
61. The Old-Avestan year seems to he considered as composed of units of time, each fifteen days or a fortnight long. This is perhaps a remnant of the earliest and primitive time-reckoning of the Iranians by half-months. Consequently the year consisted of twenty-four fortnights, arranged in groups of three, four, five, two, fire, and fire, each of the groups being one of the six seasons or yâiryas (the fourth one, however, being supplemented later by five days as epagomenæ).
62. In Yasht 7.4, there is mention of zaremaêm paiti, "when the moon brings the warmth with its light, the greenish plants shoot always towards the spring on the earth". The Pahlavi book Dadestan-i Denik, 31, 14 (West's translation) speaking of the Ardibehesht (of course, the vihêjakîk month) says that the name of this month in

religion (i.e. in Avesta) is Zaremaya and in this month the butter of mêdhiôk-zarem is produced. This expression (zaremaya raoghna = the butter of zaremaya) is also used in the verse 18 of the so-called Yasht 22 of the Avesta (SBE, iv, Darmesteter's English translation of the Avesta). That the beginning of the year or season was not on the point of the vernal equinox in the strict sense among the less advanced peoples is also to a certain extent due to the difficulty of ascertaining the time of the equinoxes by simple and ordinary means. B. is perhaps right when he asserts (AB., p. 216) that for the primitive peoples the observation of the solstices is incomparably easier than that of the equinoxes, which needs an advanced knowledge of astronomy and astronomical instruments, whereas the solstice can be found out by the simpler method of using a gnomon.

63. This festival is apparently the same as jashn-i vahâr, which was celebrated "forty-five days beyond New Year's Day at a place becoming specially noted where people went from many quarters out to the place of festival (yasno kâr)" and whereto Zoroaster has proceeded (Selections of Zadspram, West's translation, SBE, xlvii, p. 154). If this tradition is old and authentic it indicates that this festival, though comparatively of later origin, nevertheless existed in Zoroaster's time and was celebrated with full attendance. The translation of the passage of Zartusht Nameh relating to this festival by Wilson (The Parsi Religion, Bombay, 1843), however, does not agree fully with putting it in the second month of the year.

64. Exactly as the Khwarazmians of the tenth century, according to B. (AB., pp. 236, 237, and 241), used to count from the day Ajgâr (most probably in origin the Khwarazmian maidyoshahem) in both directions for fixing the seasons for all kinds of agricultural work.

65. Summer being the season of work for agricultural people, many holidays for rest were, no doubt, needed, contrary to winter, which was the off-season.

66. A parallel is to he found in the Jewish fast of `âshûrâ adopted at first by Muslims, but changed later to the month of Ramadan when their relations with the Jews became unfriendly.

67. That Nehemia's patron was the first Achaemenian king of this name and not the second is, I believe, proved by the Aramaic papyri of Elephantine cf. Schäder, Ezra der Schreiber.

68. This fast (the settlement of the court in Babylonia for more than half a century) may account for many other tendencies in the

Achaemenian empire, and perhaps among others for the adoption of the Aramaic language as the official means of correspondence in the imperial chancellery and State departments.

69. The mention of Babylon in Yasht 5.29 fits in with the removal of the seat of the government or of the court from Susa to Babylon by the first Zoroastrian king, Artaxerxes I, the Constantine of that faith. The same Yasht contains the name of Anahita, which may also increase the probability of its composition in that period.

70. Or at any rate before the first intercalation of the Persian year.

71. Cf. R. Reitzenstein, "Plato u. Zarathustra" (in Vortäge der Bibliothek Warburg, 1927) and Studien zum antiken Synkretismus, 1926, as well as H. H. Schäder in the last-named volume.

72. The mention of these deities in the inscription of Artaxerxes Mnemon or the report of Berossos about his special attachment to the same divinities does not necessarily imply that they were first recognized during the reign of this monarch, as is often held. This recognition might have taken place at any time between the unknown date of the inscription of Artaxerxes Macrocheir and that of Mnemon, unless some long inscription should be discovered belonging to the later part of the reign of the former king or from the reign of Darius Ochus, praising Ahura Mazda and ignoring Anahita, Mithra, and others.

73. As Benveniste remarks (The Persian Religion according to the chief Greek Texts, 1929), this is "the first definite mention of the name of Zoroaster in Greece". The passages attributed to Xanthus the Lydian relating to the date of the Iranian prophet or to the recalling of his words by Persians when they were going to burn Croesus are of doubtful authenticity. Even if they proved to be authentic, they would not imply the adherence of the Persian kings to Zoroastrianism, but would only suggest that Xanthus knew the name of the Iranian reformer whose new religion had gradually been spreading (westwards) in Iran for some hundred years before his time. Clemens puts the composition of Alcibiades after 374.

74. Athenseus, Deipnosophists, x, 434 (English translation by Charles Burton Gulick, 1927, bk. iv, p. 469). Duris (according to the same source) adds also the permission for the king to dance.

75. He was there apparently from 414 till 398 and wrote probably in 390.

76. The scope of this article does not permit the discussion of these

reasons here. The place of the epagomenæ indicates that the intercalation was the seventh and eighth together, and not the eighth and ninth. The next or the ninth intercalation would have fallen in AD 639, just two years after the fall of the capital of the Iranian empire on the Arab invasion, which brought to an end the national sovereignty of Persia and all its official institutions including the intercalation in their calendar.

77. SBE. v, p. 199, cf. Jackson, Zorostrian Studies, p. 162.

78. Baga, which was originally a general name for gods, seems to have become gradually the name par excellence of Mithra. The Khwarazmian name for the 16th day of the month is, according to B.'s list, Figh, which corresponds to the day of Mihr in the Persian calendar.

79. According to Stuart Jones (ERE., vol. 8, p. 752, on Mithraism), Mithra is identified with Shamash in a tablet from the library of Assurbanipal (R., iii, 69, 1, 72).

80. The Yasht, 10, however, makes Mithra almost equal in power to Ahura Mazda and the ally of the latter.

81. ERE, s.v. Festival.

82. According to Neugebauer's Hilfstafeln zur technischen Chronologie, Kiel, 1937.

83. According to a calculation based on the Zodiakaltafel of Schram.

84. We may also suppose that the 10th day of the Old-Persian month corresponded not to the 10th but to the 11th day of the Babylonian month, as a difference of one day is always possible owing, no doubt, to the different time of the first visibility of the new moon in Babylon and Hamadan. The correspondence between this day and the equinox will then be complete. Moreover, according to the narrative of Herodotus (iii, 78) Darius killed Gaumata in darkness, when he was hesitating to strike him lest Gobryas should be hit, and Ctesias (Excerpt. Pers., § 14) says that the usurper was sleeping with his Babylonian concubine. Again Herodotus says (iii, 79), that the conspirators after killing Gaumata went out and called the people to massacre the Magians..., that the slaughter continued [the whole day], and that if the night had not fallen no Magian would have been left alive. Now from all these facts it can be deduced that the day of the massacre of the Magians or Magophonia was, in fact, the day following that of the actual slaying of the usurper.

85. If we take into consideration the fact that the Persian, of the fifth century BC did not obtain in their astronomical calculation the same exact result which we have today, the possibility of their error of one day would be easily conceivable. This can account for four years difference, if the date of the adoption of the calendar was really 441 and not one or two years earlier. Strictly speaking, in 441, the 16th day of Mihr corresponded to 27th September.

86. It is true that Kugler (Sternkunde, vol. i, pp. 173–4, and several other places of this book) contests this assumption and suggests that the starting point for the division of the year into four equal parts (each 91.25 days) was the spring equinox. He is of the opinion that since the Babylonian ephemerides always used to put the vernal equinox four to five days later than its real place, the summer solstice (91.25 days after that conventional but wrong equinox day) fell a little later than the real solstice and the autumnal equinox (182.5 days later) fell incidentally quite in its right and astronomical place. But the result is, nevertheless, the same. It is even possible to suppose that the Babylonians, attaching special importance to the autumnal equinox, tried to keep that point in its strict place, and in order to effect this they placed the day they fixed for the vernal equinox a few days later, so that it would fail exactly two quarters or 182.5 days before the astronomical autumnal equinox. This peculiar arrangement, it is true, is noticed only in the cuneiform documents relating to the second century BC, but there is no reason to think that the same process was not in use in older times.

87. With the fusion of the Old-Persian and Young-Avestan calendars into one system about 441 BC, it is possible that a good many of the characteristics of the Old-Persian calendar, which was in many respects a copy of the Babylonian calendar, were incorporated into the new system. For instance, the adoption of the ordinary four seasons (not as substitutes for their own seasons but as a parallel system) may be one of the effects of this fusion. Also the Babylonian way of beginning the spring and summer some days later than the astronomical points (see the note supra) may have been followed by the Iranians, and therefore they may have considered the beginning of summer to be conventionally on 15th Tir, i.e. two days later than the real solstice.

88. If we put the date of the adoption of the new official calendar in 441 BC, the summer solstice would fall exactly on 15 Tir,

but Mihragan would preceed the autumnal equinox by one day.

89. The same process we find in the Avardadsal feast of Indian Parsis, which is celebrated now on the 6th day (the day of Hordad or Amurdad) of the month of Safendarmad (the 12th month) and which, no doubt, was created to mark the place of Nauruz in the non-intercalated (so-called Kadimi) year after the Parsis had executed an intercalation of one month in the twelfth century (see Kharegat, in Modi's Memorial Volume, p. 115).

90. The same distinction is described in Denkard, iii, see recent translation by Nyberg in his Texte zum Mazdayasnian Kalender, Uppsala, 1934, pp. 30–39.

91. At Mihragan, winter clothes were distributed by the kings, at Tiragan people bathed in the rivers, in the first and second Adar-jashn they lit fires in their houses, at Sada they used to light fires in open places, and the Khwarazmians used the civil feasts as points for the calculation of their agricultural operations even in the tenth century.

92. Or to 15th January, if we take the epagomenæ in calculation and assume it was at the end of Safendarmad.

93. AB., p. 222. The Shah-nameh of Firdausi, however, puts this event on the first day of Mihr. Had the Y.A. calendar been in use at that time, this day would have fallen in 522, only three or four days after the equinox.

94. AB., p. 220.

95. Ibid., p. 226.

96. In fact, Ram is the name of the 21st day of every Zoroastrian month, but the compound word as the name of a feast is only used for 21st of Mihr.

97. The equinox was on 28th September and the 10th day of Bâgayâdi on 3rd October.

98. Persica, § 15, and in Athenæus, x, 434 (Charles Burton Gulick's English translation, iv, 469).

99. B. attributes, this set to the Sasanian king Hormuz (Ohrmazd IV, 578–590), AB., p. 224.

100. Menander Protecter relates that the Byzantine Ambassador John sent by Justin II in 565 to Persia was obliged when on his way to the Persian court to halt for ten days in the town of Dârâ, because of the celebration in Nasîbîn of the feast of manes, which Menander calls Furdigân, or according to Causin's translation Furdiga (Histoire de

Constantinople depuis le règne de l'ancien Justin, jusqu'à la fin de l'empire, traduit sur les originaux Grecs par Mr. Causin, Paris, 1672; les Ambassades ... écrites par Menandre, Chapitre xii, p. 56). In that year third feast was certainly on 22nd February–4th March.

101. The gradual extension of the religions festivals or mourning days is not a rare thing, and there are many examples of this in Persia in the last centuries. B. says (Chronology, Istanbul MS.) that the learned men and kings of Iran have made Frawardigan the greatest of all feasts and have added to it three days more for the manifestation of their devotion, beginning it with the day Dai-pa-Den (the 23rd). In later ages this feast became still longer and according to Karkaria in Dastur Hosheng's Memorial Volume some Parsis have extended it to seventeen or eighteen days, and there was in the last century a good deal of discussion among the Parsis as to the real length of the festival.

102. The Pahlavi book, Mainog-i Khrad, which is believed to have been composed about the end of the sixth century, mentions this feast as consisting of five days.

103. However, this name indicates the antiquity of the Armenian calendar only if the Armenian Frawardigan did not remain fixed at the end of the vague year, as did the Sogdian.

104. The passages in question run as follows: "Those (the two months which are the middle of winter, the heart of winter) now are the months Bahman, and Shahrivar, that is, the heart of winter, that is it is more severe: although it is all severe, yet at that time it is more severe." I am indebted to Professor H. W. Bailey the translation of this passage. This may also indicate the age of the said commentary which should have been composed according to the above-mentioned concordance in the fifth century.

105. Unless one supposes that the occasion was the time for the eighth intercalation, that it was the turn for Aban to be repeated, that then the eighth and the ninth were effected together by repeating two months (Aban and Adar), but that the epagomenæ were moved forward only one month, i.e. to the end of the month Aban (where they ought to have been placed if there had only been one intercalation) and not to the end of Adar, as was to be expected. That such a process has taken place is not, however, easy to assume, though it is not impossible that it has. In that case the institution of the intercalation system must be put about 560 BC.

106. Journal of the K. R. Cama Oriental Institution, Bombay, 1937, p. 52.

107. This fraction of day might have been made in practice a round number of hours, i.e. six hours or a quarter of a day.

108. Both Abû Ma'shar and Kharaqî give the number in the terms of an arc of the celestial sphere, which converted into time would make the number mentioned above.

109. maidyozarem, as stated above, was in all probability the last to be introduced.

110. I follow the Zoroastrian tradition which puts the coming of the religion 258 years before Alexander's conquest of Persia, though I am aware of the controversy concerning this question.

111. It is, however, also possible, though not very probable, that this process of two successive reforms was in reverse order, i.e. that first the State and the Achaemenian court adopted the Egyptian system in place of their Old-Persian calendar and that subsequently the Zoroastrian community also adhered to it.

BIOGRAPHIES

Dr Payam Nabarz

Payam Nabarz is Persian born. He is a Sufi and a practicing Dervish, and has spent much time as a wandering Dervish walking the land. In England he has studied British Neo-Paganism among many other spiritual Traditions; while most people were heading east in search of enlightenment, he went west. The grass is always greener on the other side! He is the founder of Spirit of Peace, a charitable organization that aids various charities (in the past, Amnesty International and Adopt a Minefield). Spirit of Peace is dedicated to personal inner and world peace through interfaith dialogue between followers of different spiritual paths. Nabarz's numerous writings have appeared in many esoteric magazines including The Sufi, Touchstone (the journal of OBOD), Pagan Dawn (the journal of the Pagan Federation), Stone Circle, Silver Star, The Little Red Book, Pentacle, White Dragon and The Cauldron.

Dr T H Taqizadeh

Seyyed Hassan Taqizadeh (1878–1969) was a leading figure of the Constitutional Revolution of Iran (1907–1911). He had an active socio-political life and was elected to the parliament as a representative of the people of Tabriz in 1924. He published the Kaveh newspaper in Berlin. He was recognized as a prominent scholar in the field of calendar systems and Iranian studies both in Iran and Europe. The significant of Taqizadeh's work is that he succeeded in changing the country's calendar system from lunar to solar after thirteen centuries.

Appendix. Gregorian calendar conversion to Persian calendar.

There are four Zoroastrian based calendars, Shehenshahi, Kadmi, Fasli, and Zoroastrian Religious Era (ZRE). For the purpose of the Mar-Nameh the ZRE calendar format is used as it the calendar which became popular with many Zoroastrians in India, Iran and other countries.

The following are the calendars for 2006 to 2008. On the day a snake is seen in real life, or a dream, then look in the number / day column in the Persian ZRE calendar below for the meaning. Then, look at the corresponding day in chapter 4. For example, if you dreamt of or saw a snake on the 2nd of January 2006. This was day 16 in the Persian calendar, hence looking in chapter 4, couplet number 16, it says: "you will on a journey sooner than later".

The following calendars were calculated using 'Zcal' programme from Avesta.org. The names are modified for ease of reading.

Calendar year 2006 converted to the Zoroastrian calendar year 3743.

2006 AD	Z. R. E. 3743 - 3744 ZRE
Jan-1-2006-Sun	11 Dai (Day 287) 3743 ZRE
Jan-2-2006-Mon	12 Dai (Day 288)
Jan-3-2006-Tue	13 Dai (Day 289)
Jan-4-2006-Wed	14 Dai (Day 290)
Jan-5-2006-Thu	15 Dai (Day 291)
Jan-6-2006-Fri	16 Dai (Day 292)
Jan-7-2006-Sat	17 Dai (Day 293)
Jan-8-2006-Sun	18 Dai (Day 294)
Jan-9-2006-Mon	19 Dai (Day 295)
Jan-10-2006-Tue	20 Dai (Day 296)
Jan-11-2006-Wed	21 Dai (Day 297)
Jan-12-2006-Thu	22 Dai (Day 298)
Jan-13-2006-Fri	23 Dai (Day 299)
Jan-14-2006-Sat	24 Dai (Day 300)
Jan-15-2006-Sun	25 Dai (Day 301)
Jan-16-2006-Mon	26 Dai (Day 302)
Jan-17-2006-Tue	27 Dai (Day 303)
Jan-18-2006-Wed	28 Dai (Day 304)
Jan-19-2006-Thu	29 Dai (Day 305)

Jan-20-2006-Fri	30 Dai (Day 306)
Jan-21-2006-Sat	**1 Bahman (Day 307) 3743 ZRE**
Jan-22-2006-Sun	2 Bahman (Day 308)
Jan-23-2006-Mon	3 Bahman (Day 309)
Jan-24-2006-Tue	4 Bahman (Day 310)
Jan-25-2006-Wed	5 Bahman (Day 311)
Jan-26-2006-Thu	6 Bahman (Day 312)
Jan-27-2006-Fri	7 Bahman (Day 313)
Jan-28-2006-Sat	8 Bahman (Day 314)
Jan-29-2006-Sun	9 Bahman (Day 315)
Jan-30-2006-Mon	10 Bahman (Day 316)
Jan-31-2006-Tue	11 Bahman (Day 317)
Feb-1-2006-Wed	12 Bahman (Day 318)
Feb-2-2006-Thu	13 Bahman (Day 319)
Feb-3-2006-Fri	14 Bahman (Day 320)
Feb-4-2006-Sat	15 Bahman (Day 321)
Feb-5-2006-Sun	16 Bahman (Day 322)
Feb-6-2006-Mon	17 Bahman (Day 323)
Feb-7-2006-Tue	18 Bahman (Day 324)
Feb-8-2006-Wed	19 Bahman (Day 325)
Feb-9-2006-Thu	20 Bahman (Day 326)
Feb-10-2006-Fri	21 Bahman (Day 327)
Feb-11-2006-Sat	22 Bahman (Day 328)
Feb-12-2006-Sun	23 Bahman (Day 329)
Feb-13-2006-Mon	24 Bahman (Day 330)
Feb-14-2006-Tue	25 Bahman (Day 331)
Feb-15-2006-Wed	26 Bahman (Day 332)
Feb-16-2006-Thu	27 Bahman (Day 333)
Feb-17-2006-Fri	28 Bahman (Day 334)
Feb-18-2006-Sat	29 Bahman (Day 335)
Feb-19-2006-Sun	30 Bahman (Day 336)
Feb-20-2006-Mon	**1 Esfand(armaz) (Day 337) 3743 ZRE**
Feb-21-2006-Tue	2 Esfand(armaz) (Day 338)
Feb-22-2006-Wed	3 Esfand(armaz) (Day 339)
Feb-23-2006-Thu	4 Esfand(armaz) (Day 340)
Feb-24-2006-Fri	5 Esfand(armaz) (Day 341)
Feb-25-2006-Sat	6 Esfand(armaz) (Day 342)
Feb-26-2006-Sun	7 Esfand(armaz) (Day 343)
Feb-27-2006-Mon	8 Esfand(armaz) (Day 344)
Feb-28-2006-Tue	9 Esfand(armaz) (Day 345)
Mar-1-2006-Wed	10 Esfand(armaz) (Day 346)
Mar-2-2006-Thu	11 Esfand(armaz) (Day 347)

Mar-3-2006-Fri	12 Esfand(armaz) (Day 348)
Mar-4-2006-Sat	13 Esfand(armaz) (Day 349)
Mar-5-2006-Sun	14 Esfand(armaz) (Day 350)
Mar-6-2006-Mon	15 Esfand(armaz) (Day 351)
Mar-7-2006-Tue	16 Esfand(armaz) (Day 352)
Mar-8-2006-Wed	17 Esfand(armaz) (Day 353)
Mar-9-2006-Thu	18 Esfand(armaz) (Day 354)
Mar-10-2006-Fri	19 Esfand(armaz) (Day 355)
Mar-11-2006-Sat	20 Esfand(armaz) (Day 356)
Mar-12-2006-Sun	21 Esfand(armaz) (Day 357)
Mar-13-2006-Mon	22 Esfand(armaz) (Day 358)
Mar-14-2006-Tue	23 Esfand(armaz) (Day 359)
Mar-15-2006-Wed	24 Esfand(armaz) (Day 360)
Mar-16-2006-Thu	25 Esfand(armaz) (Day 361)
Mar-17-2006-Fri	26 Esfand(armaz) (Day 362)
Mar-18-2006-Sat	27 Esfand(armaz) (Day 363)
Mar-19-2006-Sun	28 Esfand(armaz) (Day 364)
Mar-20-2006-Mon	29 Esfand(armaz) (Day 365)
Mar-21-2006-Tue	**1 Farvardeen(Day 1) 3744 ZRE**
Mar-22-2006-Wed	2 Farvardeen(Day 2)
Mar-23-2006-Thu	3 Farvardeen(Day 3)
Mar-24-2006-Fri	4 Farvardeen(Day 4)
Mar-25-2006-Sat	5 Farvardeen(Day 5)
Mar-26-2006-Sun	6 Farvardeen(Day 6)
Mar-27-2006-Mon	7 Farvardeen(Day 7)
Mar-28-2006-Tue	8 Farvardeen(Day 8)
Mar-29-2006-Wed	9 Farvardeen(Day 9)
Mar-30-2006-Thu	10 Farvardeen(Day 10)
Mar-31-2006-Fri	11 Farvardeen(Day 11)
Apr-1-2006-Sat	12 Farvardeen(Day 12)
Apr-2-2006-Sun	13 Farvardeen(Day 13)
Apr-3-2006-Mon	14 Farvardeen(Day 14)
Apr-4-2006-Tue	15 Farvardeen(Day 15)
Apr-5-2006-Wed	16 Farvardeen(Day 16)
Apr-6-2006-Thu	17 Farvardeen(Day 17)
Apr-7-2006-Fri	18 Farvardeen(Day 18)
Apr-8-2006-Sat	19 Farvardeen(Day 19)
Apr-9-2006-Sun	20 Farvardeen(Day 20)
Apr-10-2006-Mon	21 Farvardeen(Day 21)
Apr-11-2006-Tue	22 Farvardeen(Day 22)
Apr-12-2006-Wed	23 Farvardeen(Day 23)
Apr-13-2006-Thu	24 Farvardeen(Day 24)

Apr-14-2006-Fri	25 Farvardeen(Day 25)
Apr-15-2006-Sat	26 Farvardeen(Day 26)
Apr-16-2006-Sun	27 Farvardeen(Day 27)
Apr-17-2006-Mon	28 Farvardeen(Day 28)
Apr-18-2006-Tue	29 Farvardeen(Day 29)
Apr-19-2006-Wed	30 Farvardeen(Day 30)
Apr-20-2006-Thu	31 Farvardeen(Day 31)
Apr-21-2006-Fri	**1 Ardibehesht (Day 32) 3744 ZRE**
Apr-22-2006-Sat	2 Ardibehesht (Day 33)
Apr-23-2006-Sun	3 Ardibehesht (Day 34)
Apr-24-2006-Mon	4 Ardibehesht (Day 35)
Apr-25-2006-Tue	5 Ardibehesht (Day 36)
Apr-26-2006-Wed	6 Ardibehesht (Day 37)
Apr-27-2006-Thu	7 Ardibehesht (Day 38)
Apr-28-2006-Fri	8 Ardibehesht (Day 39)
Apr-29-2006-Sat	9 Ardibehesht (Day 40)
Apr-30-2006-Sun	10 Ardibehesht (Day 41)
May-1-2006-Mon	11 Ardibehesht (Day 42)
May-2-2006-Tue	12 Ardibehesht (Day 43)
May-3-2006-Wed	13 Ardibehesht (Day 44)
May-4-2006-Thu	14 Ardibehesht (Day 45)
May-5-2006-Fri	15 Ardibehesht (Day 46)
May-6-2006-Sat	16 Ardibehesht (Day 47)
May-7-2006-Sun	17 Ardibehesht (Day 48)
May-8-2006-Mon	18 Ardibehesht (Day 49)
May-9-2006-Tue	19 Ardibehesht (Day 50)
May-10-2006-Wed	20 Ardibehesht (Day 51)
May-11-2006-Thu	21 Ardibehesht (Day 52)
May-12-2006-Fri	22 Ardibehesht (Day 53)
May-13-2006-Sat	23 Ardibehesht (Day 54)
May-14-2006-Sun	24 Ardibehesht (Day 55)
May-15-2006-Mon	25 Ardibehesht (Day 56)
May-16-2006-Tue	26 Ardibehesht (Day 57)
May-17-2006-Wed	27 Ardibehesht (Day 58)
May-18-2006-Thu	28 Ardibehesht (Day 59)
May-19-2006-Fri	29 Ardibehesht (Day 60)
May-20-2006-Sat	30 Ardibehesht (Day 61)
May-21-2006-Sun	31 Ardibehesht (Day 62)
May-22-2006-Mon	**1 Khordad (Day 63) 3744 ZRE**
May-23-2006-Tue	2 Khordad (Day 64)
May-24-2006-Wed	3 Khordad (Day 65)
May-25-2006-Thu	4 Khordad (Day 66)

May-26-2006-Fri	5 Khordad (Day 67)
May-27-2006-Sat	6 Khordad (Day 68)
May-28-2006-Sun	7 Khordad (Day 69)
May-29-2006-Mon	8 Khordad (Day 70)
May-30-2006-Tue	9 Khordad (Day 71)
May-31-2006-Wed	10 Khordad (Day 72)
Jun-1-2006-Thu	11 Khordad (Day 73)
Jun-2-2006-Fri	12 Khordad (Day 74)
Jun-3-2006-Sat	13 Khordad (Day 75)
Jun-4-2006-Sun	14 Khordad (Day 76)
Jun-5-2006-Mon	15 Khordad (Day 77)
Jun-6-2006-Tue	16 Khordad (Day 78)
Jun-7-2006-Wed	17 Khordad (Day 79)
Jun-8-2006-Thu	18 Khordad (Day 80)
Jun-9-2006-Fri	19 Khordad (Day 81)
Jun-10-2006-Sat	20 Khordad (Day 82)
Jun-11-2006-Sun	21 Khordad (Day 83)
Jun-12-2006-Mon	22 Khordad (Day 84)
Jun-13-2006-Tue	23 Khordad (Day 85)
Jun-14-2006-Wed	24 Khordad (Day 86)
Jun-15-2006-Thu	25 Khordad (Day 87)
Jun-16-2006-Fri	26 Khordad (Day 88)
Jun-17-2006-Sat	27 Khordad (Day 89)
Jun-18-2006-Sun	28 Khordad (Day 90)
Jun-19-2006-Mon	29 Khordad (Day 91)
Jun-20-2006-Tue	30 Khordad (Day 92)
Jun-21-2006-Wed	31 Khordad (Day 93)
Jun-22-2006-Thu	**1 Tir (Day 94) 3744 ZRE**
Jun-23-2006-Fri	2 Tir (Day 95)
Jun-24-2006-Sat	3 Tir (Day 96)
Jun-25-2006-Sun	4 Tir (Day 97)
Jun-26-2006-Mon	5 Tir (Day 98)
Jun-27-2006-Tue	6 Tir (Day 99)
Jun-28-2006-Wed	7 Tir (Day 100)
Jun-29-2006-Thu	8 Tir (Day 101)
Jun-30-2006-Fri	9 Tir (Day 102)
Jul-1-2006-Sat	10 Tir (Day 103)
Jul-2-2006-Sun	11 Tir (Day 104)
Jul-3-2006-Mon	12 Tir (Day 105)
Jul-4-2006-Tue	13 Tir (Day 106)
Jul-5-2006-Wed	14 Tir (Day 107)
Jul-6-2006-Thu	15 Tir (Day 108)

Jul-7-2006-Fri	16 Tir (Day 109)
Jul-8-2006-Sat	17 Tir (Day 110)
Jul-9-2006-Sun	18 Tir (Day 111)
Jul-10-2006-Mon	19 Tir (Day 112)
Jul-11-2006-Tue	20 Tir (Day 113)
Jul-12-2006-Wed	21 Tir (Day 114)
Jul-13-2006-Thu	22 Tir (Day 115)
Jul-14-2006-Fri	23 Tir (Day 116)
Jul-15-2006-Sat	24 Tir (Day 117)
Jul-16-2006-Sun	25 Tir (Day 118)
Jul-17-2006-Mon	26 Tir (Day 119)
Jul-18-2006-Tue	27 Tir (Day 120)
Jul-19-2006-Wed	28 Tir (Day 121)
Jul-20-2006-Thu	29 Tir (Day 122)
Jul-21-2006-Fri	30 Tir (Day 123)
Jul-22-2006-Sat	31 Tir (Day 124)
Jul-23-2006-Sun	**1 Amordad (Day 125) 3744 ZRE**
Jul-24-2006-Mon	2 Amordad (Day 126)
Jul-25-2006-Tue	3 Amordad (Day 127)
Jul-26-2006-Wed	4 Amordad (Day 128)
Jul-27-2006-Thu	5 Amordad (Day 129)
Jul-28-2006-Fri	6 Amordad (Day 130)
Jul-29-2006-Sat	7 Amordad (Day 131)
Jul-30-2006-Sun	8 Amordad (Day 132)
Jul-31-2006-Mon	9 Amordad (Day 133)
Aug-1-2006-Tue	10 Amordad (Day 134)
Aug-2-2006-Wed	11 Amordad (Day 135)
Aug-3-2006-Thu	12 Amordad (Day 136)
Aug-4-2006-Fri	13 Amordad (Day 137)
Aug-5-2006-Sat	14 Amordad (Day 138)
Aug-6-2006-Sun	15 Amordad (Day 139)
Aug-7-2006-Mon	16 Amordad (Day 140)
Aug-8-2006-Tue	17 Amordad (Day 141)
Aug-9-2006-Wed	18 Amordad (Day 142)
Aug-10-2006-Thu	19 Amordad (Day 143)
Aug-11-2006-Fri	20 Amordad (Day 144)
Aug-12-2006-Sat	21 Amordad (Day 145)
Aug-13-2006-Sun	22 Amordad (Day 146)
Aug-14-2006-Mon	23 Amordad (Day 147)
Aug-15-2006-Tue	24 Amordad (Day 148)
Aug-16-2006-Wed	25 Amordad (Day 149)
Aug-17-2006-Thu	26 Amordad (Day 150)

Aug-18-2006-Fri	27 Amordad (Day 151)
Aug-19-2006-Sat	28 Amordad (Day 152)
Aug-20-2006-Sun	29 Amordad (Day 153)
Aug-21-2006-Mon	30 Amordad (Day 154)
Aug-22-2006-Tue	31 Amordad (Day 155)
Aug-23-2006-Wed	**1 Shahrivar (Day 156) 3744 ZRE**
Aug-24-2006-Thu	2 Shahrivar (Day 157)
Aug-25-2006-Fri	3 Shahrivar (Day 158)
Aug-26-2006-Sat	4 Shahrivar (Day 159)
Aug-27-2006-Sun	5 Shahrivar (Day 160)
Aug-28-2006-Mon	6 Shahrivar (Day 161)
Aug-29-2006-Tue	7 Shahrivar (Day 162)
Aug-30-2006-Wed	8 Shahrivar (Day 163)
Aug-31-2006-Thu	9 Shahrivar (Day 164)
Sep-1-2006-Fri	10 Shahrivar (Day 165)
Sep-2-2006-Sat	11 Shahrivar (Day 166)
Sep-3-2006-Sun	12 Shahrivar (Day 167)
Sep-4-2006-Mon	13 Shahrivar (Day 168)
Sep-5-2006-Tue	14 Shahrivar (Day 169)
Sep-6-2006-Wed	15 Shahrivar (Day 170)
Sep-7-2006-Thu	16 Shahrivar (Day 171)
Sep-8-2006-Fri	17 Shahrivar (Day 172)
Sep-9-2006-Sat	18 Shahrivar (Day 173)
Sep-10-2006-Sun	19 Shahrivar (Day 174)
Sep-11-2006-Mon	20 Shahrivar (Day 175)
Sep-12-2006-Tue	21 Shahrivar (Day 176)
Sep-13-2006-Wed	22 Shahrivar (Day 177)
Sep-14-2006-Thu	23 Shahrivar (Day 178)
Sep-15-2006-Fri	24 Shahrivar (Day 179)
Sep-16-2006-Sat	25 Shahrivar (Day 180)
Sep-17-2006-Sun	26 Shahrivar (Day 181)
Sep-18-2006-Mon	27 Shahrivar (Day 182)
Sep-19-2006-Tue	28 Shahrivar (Day 183)
Sep-20-2006-Wed	29 Shahrivar (Day 184)
Sep-21-2006-Thu	30 Shahrivar (Day 185)
Sep-22-2006-Fri	31 Shahrivar (Day 186)
Sep-23-2006-Sat	**1 Mehr (Day 187) 3744 ZRE**
Sep-24-2006-Sun	2 Mehr (Day 188)
Sep-25-2006-Mon	3 Mehr (Day 189)
Sep-26-2006-Tue	4 Mehr (Day 190)
Sep-27-2006-Wed	5 Mehr (Day 191)
Sep-28-2006-Thu	6 Mehr (Day 192)

Sep-29-2006-Fri	7 Mehr (Day 193)
Sep-30-2006-Sat	8 Mehr (Day 194)
Oct-1-2006-Sun	9 Mehr (Day 195)
Oct-2-2006-Mon	10 Mehr (Day 196)
Oct-3-2006-Tue	11 Mehr (Day 197)
Oct-4-2006-Wed	12 Mehr (Day 198)
Oct-5-2006-Thu	13 Mehr (Day 199)
Oct-6-2006-Fri	14 Mehr (Day 200)
Oct-7-2006-Sat	15 Mehr (Day 201)
Oct-8-2006-Sun	16 Mehr (Day 202)
Oct-9-2006-Mon	17 Mehr (Day 203)
Oct-10-2006-Tue	18 Mehr (Day 204)
Oct-11-2006-Wed	19 Mehr (Day 205)
Oct-12-2006-Thu	20 Mehr (Day 206)
Oct-13-2006-Fri	21 Mehr (Day 207)
Oct-14-2006-Sat	22 Mehr (Day 208)
Oct-15-2006-Sun	23 Mehr (Day 209)
Oct-16-2006-Mon	24 Mehr (Day 210)
Oct-17-2006-Tue	25 Mehr (Day 211)
Oct-18-2006-Wed	26 Mehr (Day 212)
Oct-19-2006-Thu	27 Mehr (Day 213)
Oct-20-2006-Fri	28 Mehr (Day 214)
Oct-21-2006-Sat	29 Mehr (Day 215)
Oct-22-2006-Sun	30 Mehr (Day 216)
Oct-23-2006-Mon	**1 Aban (Day 217) 3744 ZRE**
Oct-24-2006-Tue	2 Aban (Day 218)
Oct-25-2006-Wed	3 Aban (Day 219)
Oct-26-2006-Thu	4 Aban (Day 220)
Oct-27-2006-Fri	5 Aban (Day 221)
Oct-28-2006-Sat	6 Aban (Day 222)
Oct-29-2006-Sun	7 Aban (Day 223)
Oct-30-2006-Mon	8 Aban (Day 224)
Oct-31-2006-Tue	9 Aban (Day 225)
Nov-1-2006-Wed	10 Aban (Day 226)
Nov-2-2006-Thu	11 Aban (Day 227)
Nov-3-2006-Fri	12 Aban (Day 228)
Nov-4-2006-Sat	13 Aban (Day 229)
Nov-5-2006-Sun	14 Aban (Day 230)
Nov-6-2006-Mon	15 Aban (Day 231)
Nov-7-2006-Tue	16 Aban (Day 232)
Nov-8-2006-Wed	17 Aban (Day 233)
Nov-9-2006-Thu	18 Aban (Day 234)

Nov-10-2006-Fri	19 Aban (Day 235)
Nov-11-2006-Sat	20 Aban (Day 236)
Nov-12-2006-Sun	21 Aban (Day 237)
Nov-13-2006-Mon	22 Aban (Day 238)
Nov-14-2006-Tue	23 Aban (Day 239)
Nov-15-2006-Wed	24 Aban (Day 240)
Nov-16-2006-Thu	25 Aban (Day 241)
Nov-17-2006-Fri	26 Aban (Day 242)
Nov-18-2006-Sat	27 Aban (Day 243)
Nov-19-2006-Sun	28 Aban (Day 244)
Nov-20-2006-Mon	29 Aban (Day 245)
Nov-21-2006-Tue	30 Aban (Day 246)
Nov-22-2006-Wed	**1 Azar (Day 247) 3744 ZRE**
Nov-23-2006-Thu	2 Azar (Day 248)
Nov-24-2006-Fri	3 Azar (Day 249)
Nov-25-2006-Sat	4 Azar (Day 250)
Nov-26-2006-Sun	5 Azar (Day 251)
Nov-27-2006-Mon	6 Azar (Day 252)
Nov-28-2006-Tue	7 Azar (Day 253)
Nov-29-2006-Wed	8 Azar (Day 254)
Nov-30-2006-Thu	9 Azar (Day 255)
Dec-1-2006-Fri	10 Azar (Day 256)
Dec-2-2006-Sat	11 Azar (Day 257)
Dec-3-2006-Sun	12 Azar (Day 258)
Dec-4-2006-Mon	13 Azar (Day 259)
Dec-5-2006-Tue	14 Azar (Day 260)
Dec-6-2006-Wed	15 Azar (Day 261)
Dec-7-2006-Thu	16 Azar (Day 262)
Dec-8-2006-Fri	17 Azar (Day 263)
Dec-9-2006-Sat	18 Azar (Day 264)
Dec-10-2006-Sun	19 Azar (Day 265)
Dec-11-2006-Mon	20 Azar (Day 266)
Dec-12-2006-Tue	21 Azar (Day 267)
Dec-13-2006-Wed	22 Azar (Day 268)
Dec-14-2006-Thu	23 Azar (Day 269)
Dec-15-2006-Fri	24 Azar (Day 270)
Dec-16-2006-Sat	25 Azar (Day 271)
Dec-17-2006-Sun	26 Azar (Day 272)
Dec-18-2006-Mon	27 Azar (Day 273)
Dec-19-2006-Tue	28 Azar (Day 274)
Dec-20-2006-Wed	29 Azar (Day 275)
Dec-21-2006-Thu	30 Azar (Day 276)

Dec-22-2006-Fri	**1 Dai (Day 277) 3744 ZRE**
Dec-23-2006-Sat	2 Dai (Day 278)
Dec-24-2006-Sun	3 Dai (Day 279)
Dec-25-2006-Mon	4 Dai (Day 280)
Dec-26-2006-Tue	5 Dai (Day 281)
Dec-27-2006-Wed	6 Dai (Day 282)
Dec-28-2006-Thu	7 Dai (Day 283)
Dec-29-2006-Fri	8 Dai (Day 284)
Dec-30-2006-Sat	9 Dai (Day 285)
Dec-31-2006-Sun	**10 Dai (Day 286) 3744 ZRE**

Calendar year 2007 converted to the Zoroastrian calendar year 3744.

2007 AD	Z. R. E. 3744 - 3745 ZRE
Jan-1-2007-Mon	**11 Dai (Day 287) 3744 ZRE**
Jan-2-2007-Tue	12 Dai (Day 288)
Jan-3-2007-Wed	13 Dai (Day 289)
Jan-4-2007-Thu	14 Dai (Day 290)
Jan-5-2007-Fri	15 Dai (Day 291)
Jan-6-2007-Sat	16 Dai (Day 292)
Jan-7-2007-Sun	17 Dai (Day 293)
Jan-8-2007-Mon	18 Dai (Day 294)
Jan-9-2007-Tue	19 Dai (Day 295)
Jan-10-2007-Wed	20 Dai (Day 296)
Jan-11-2007-Thu	21 Dai (Day 297)
Jan-12-2007-Fri	22 Dai (Day 298)
Jan-13-2007-Sat	23 Dai (Day 299)
Jan-14-2007-Sun	24 Dai (Day 300)
Jan-15-2007-Mon	25 Dai (Day 301)
Jan-16-2007-Tue	26 Dai (Day 302)
Jan-17-2007-Wed	27 Dai (Day 303)
Jan-18-2007-Thu	28 Dai (Day 304)
Jan-19-2007-Fri	29 Dai (Day 305)
Jan-20-2007-Sat	30 Dai (Day 306)
Jan-21-2007-Sun	**1 Bahman (Day 307) 3744 ZRE**
Jan-22-2007-Mon	2 Bahman (Day 308)
Jan-23-2007-Tue	3 Bahman (Day 309)
Jan-24-2007-Wed	4 Bahman (Day 310)
Jan-25-2007-Thu	5 Bahman (Day 311)
Jan-26-2007-Fri	6 Bahman (Day 312)

Jan-27-2007-Sat	7 Bahman (Day 313)
Jan-28-2007-Sun	8 Bahman (Day 314)
Jan-29-2007-Mon	9 Bahman (Day 315)
Jan-30-2007-Tue	10 Bahman (Day 316)
Jan-31-2007-Wed	11 Bahman (Day 317)
Feb-1-2007-Thu	12 Bahman (Day 318)
Feb-2-2007-Fri	13 Bahman (Day 319)
Feb-3-2007-Sat	14 Bahman (Day 320)
Feb-4-2007-Sun	15 Bahman (Day 321)
Feb-5-2007-Mon	16 Bahman (Day 322)
Feb-6-2007-Tue	17 Bahman (Day 323)
Feb-7-2007-Wed	18 Bahman (Day 324)
Feb-8-2007-Thu	19 Bahman (Day 325)
Feb-9-2007-Fri	20 Bahman (Day 326)
Feb-10-2007-Sat	21 Bahman (Day 327)
Feb-11-2007-Sun	22 Bahman (Day 328)
Feb-12-2007-Mon	23 Bahman (Day 329)
Feb-13-2007-Tue	24 Bahman (Day 330)
Feb-14-2007-Wed	25 Bahman (Day 331)
Feb-15-2007-Thu	26 Bahman (Day 332)
Feb-16-2007-Fri	27 Bahman (Day 333)
Feb-17-2007-Sat	28 Bahman (Day 334)
Feb-18-2007-Sun	29 Bahman (Day 335)
Feb-19-2007-Mon	30 Bahman (Day 336)
Feb-20-2007-Tue	**1 Esfand(armaz) (Day 337) 3744 ZRE**
Feb-21-2007-Wed	2 Esfand(armaz) (Day 338)
Feb-22-2007-Thu	3 Esfand(armaz) (Day 339)
Feb-23-2007-Fri	4 Esfand(armaz) (Day 340)
Feb-24-2007-Sat	5 Esfand(armaz) (Day 341)
Feb-25-2007-Sun	6 Esfand(armaz) (Day 342)
Feb-26-2007-Mon	7 Esfand(armaz) (Day 343)
Feb-27-2007-Tue	8 Esfand(armaz) (Day 344)
Feb-28-2007-Wed	9 Esfand(armaz) (Day 345)
Mar-1-2007-Thu	10 Esfand(armaz) (Day 346)
Mar-2-2007-Fri	11 Esfand(armaz) (Day 347)
Mar-3-2007-Sat	12 Esfand(armaz) (Day 348)
Mar-4-2007-Sun	13 Esfand(armaz) (Day 349)
Mar-5-2007-Mon	14 Esfand(armaz) (Day 350)
Mar-6-2007-Tue	15 Esfand(armaz) (Day 351)
Mar-7-2007-Wed	16 Esfand(armaz) (Day 352)
Mar-8-2007-Thu	17 Esfand(armaz) (Day 353)
Mar-9-2007-Fri	18 Esfand(armaz) (Day 354)

Mar-10-2007-Sat	19 Esfand(armaz) (Day 355)
Mar-11-2007-Sun	20 Esfand(armaz) (Day 356)
Mar-12-2007-Mon	21 Esfand(armaz) (Day 357)
Mar-13-2007-Tue	22 Esfand(armaz) (Day 358)
Mar-14-2007-Wed	23 Esfand(armaz) (Day 359)
Mar-15-2007-Thu	24 Esfand(armaz) (Day 360)
Mar-16-2007-Fri	25 Esfand(armaz) (Day 361)
Mar-17-2007-Sat	26 Esfand(armaz) (Day 362)
Mar-18-2007-Sun	27 Esfand(armaz) (Day 363)
Mar-19-2007-Mon	28 Esfand(armaz) (Day 364)
Mar-20-2007-Tue	29 Esfand(armaz) (Day 365)
Mar-21-2007-Wed	**1 Farvardeen(Day 1) 3745 ZRE**
Mar-22-2007-Thu	2 Farvardeen(Day 2)
Mar-23-2007-Fri	3 Farvardeen(Day 3)
Mar-24-2007-Sat	4 Farvardeen(Day 4)
Mar-25-2007-Sun	5 Farvardeen(Day 5)
Mar-26-2007-Mon	6 Farvardeen(Day 6)
Mar-27-2007-Tue	7 Farvardeen(Day 7)
Mar-28-2007-Wed	8 Farvardeen(Day 8)
Mar-29-2007-Thu	9 Farvardeen(Day 9)
Mar-30-2007-Fri	10 Farvardeen(Day 10)
Mar-31-2007-Sat	11 Farvardeen(Day 11)
Apr-1-2007-Sun	12 Farvardeen(Day 12)
Apr-2-2007-Mon	13 Farvardeen(Day 13)
Apr-3-2007-Tue	14 Farvardeen(Day 14)
Apr-4-2007-Wed	15 Farvardeen(Day 15)
Apr-5-2007-Thu	16 Farvardeen(Day 16)
Apr-6-2007-Fri	17 Farvardeen(Day 17)
Apr-7-2007-Sat	18 Farvardeen(Day 18)
Apr-8-2007-Sun	19 Farvardeen(Day 19)
Apr-9-2007-Mon	20 Farvardeen(Day 20)
Apr-10-2007-Tue	21 Farvardeen(Day 21)
Apr-11-2007-Wed	22 Farvardeen(Day 22)
Apr-12-2007-Thu	23 Farvardeen(Day 23)
Apr-13-2007-Fri	24 Farvardeen(Day 24)
Apr-14-2007-Sat	25 Farvardeen(Day 25)
Apr-15-2007-Sun	26 Farvardeen(Day 26)
Apr-16-2007-Mon	27 Farvardeen(Day 27)
Apr-17-2007-Tue	28 Farvardeen(Day 28)
Apr-18-2007-Wed	29 Farvardeen(Day 29)
Apr-19-2007-Thu	30 Farvardeen(Day 30)
Apr-20-2007-Fri	31 Farvardeen(Day 31)

Apr-21-2007-Sat	**1 Ardibehesht (Day 32) 3745 ZRE**
Apr-22-2007-Sun	2 Ardibehesht (Day 33)
Apr-23-2007-Mon	3 Ardibehesht (Day 34)
Apr-24-2007-Tue	4 Ardibehesht (Day 35)
Apr-25-2007-Wed	5 Ardibehesht (Day 36)
Apr-26-2007-Thu	6 Ardibehesht (Day 37)
Apr-27-2007-Fri	7 Ardibehesht (Day 38)
Apr-28-2007-Sat	8 Ardibehesht (Day 39)
Apr-29-2007-Sun	9 Ardibehesht (Day 40)
Apr-30-2007-Mon	10 Ardibehesht (Day 41)
May-1-2007-Tue	11 Ardibehesht (Day 42)
May-2-2007-Wed	12 Ardibehesht (Day 43)
May-3-2007-Thu	13 Ardibehesht (Day 44)
May-4-2007-Fri	14 Ardibehesht (Day 45)
May-5-2007-Sat	15 Ardibehesht (Day 46)
May-6-2007-Sun	16 Ardibehesht (Day 47)
May-7-2007-Mon	17 Ardibehesht (Day 48)
May-8-2007-Tue	18 Ardibehesht (Day 49)
May-9-2007-Wed	19 Ardibehesht (Day 50)
May-10-2007-Thu	20 Ardibehesht (Day 51)
May-11-2007-Fri	21 Ardibehesht (Day 52)
May-12-2007-Sat	22 Ardibehesht (Day 53)
May-13-2007-Sun	23 Ardibehesht (Day 54)
May-14-2007-Mon	24 Ardibehesht (Day 55)
May-15-2007-Tue	25 Ardibehesht (Day 56)
May-16-2007-Wed	26 Ardibehesht (Day 57)
May-17-2007-Thu	27 Ardibehesht (Day 58)
May-18-2007-Fri	28 Ardibehesht (Day 59)
May-19-2007-Sat	29 Ardibehesht (Day 60)
May-20-2007-Sun	30 Ardibehesht (Day 61)
May-21-2007-Mon	31 Ardibehesht (Day 62)
May-22-2007-Tue	**1 Khordad (Day 63) 3745 ZRE**
May-23-2007-Wed	2 Khordad (Day 64)
May-24-2007-Thu	3 Khordad (Day 65)
May-25-2007-Fri	4 Khordad (Day 66)
May-26-2007-Sat	5 Khordad (Day 67)
May-27-2007-Sun	6 Khordad (Day 68)
May-28-2007-Mon	7 Khordad (Day 69)
May-29-2007-Tue	8 Khordad (Day 70)
May-30-2007-Wed	9 Khordad (Day 71)
May-31-2007-Thu	10 Khordad (Day 72)
Jun-1-2007-Fri	11 Khordad (Day 73)

Jun-2-2007-Sat	12 Khordad (Day 74)
Jun-3-2007-Sun	13 Khordad (Day 75)
Jun-4-2007-Mon	14 Khordad (Day 76)
Jun-5-2007-Tue	15 Khordad (Day 77)
Jun-6-2007-Wed	16 Khordad (Day 78)
Jun-7-2007-Thu	17 Khordad (Day 79)
Jun-8-2007-Fri	18 Khordad (Day 80)
Jun-9-2007-Sat	19 Khordad (Day 81)
Jun-10-2007-Sun	20 Khordad (Day 82)
Jun-11-2007-Mon	21 Khordad (Day 83)
Jun-12-2007-Tue	22 Khordad (Day 84)
Jun-13-2007-Wed	23 Khordad (Day 85)
Jun-14-2007-Thu	24 Khordad (Day 86)
Jun-15-2007-Fri	25 Khordad (Day 87)
Jun-16-2007-Sat	26 Khordad (Day 88)
Jun-17-2007-Sun	27 Khordad (Day 89)
Jun-18-2007-Mon	28 Khordad (Day 90)
Jun-19-2007-Tue	29 Khordad (Day 91)
Jun-20-2007-Wed	30 Khordad (Day 92)
Jun-21-2007-Thu	31 Khordad (Day 93)
Jun-22-2007-Fri	**1 Tir (Day 94) 3745 ZRE**
Jun-23-2007-Sat	2 Tir (Day 95)
Jun-24-2007-Sun	3 Tir (Day 96)
Jun-25-2007-Mon	4 Tir (Day 97)
Jun-26-2007-Tue	5 Tir (Day 98)
Jun-27-2007-Wed	6 Tir (Day 99)
Jun-28-2007-Thu	7 Tir (Day 100)
Jun-29-2007-Fri	8 Tir (Day 101)
Jun-30-2007-Sat	9 Tir (Day 102)
Jul-1-2007-Sun	10 Tir (Day 103)
Jul-2-2007-Mon	11 Tir (Day 104)
Jul-3-2007-Tue	12 Tir (Day 105)
Jul-4-2007-Wed	13 Tir (Day 106)
Jul-5-2007-Thu	14 Tir (Day 107)
Jul-6-2007-Fri	15 Tir (Day 108)
Jul-7-2007-Sat	16 Tir (Day 109)
Jul-8-2007-Sun	17 Tir (Day 110)
Jul-9-2007-Mon	18 Tir (Day 111)
Jul-10-2007-Tue	19 Tir (Day 112)
Jul-11-2007-Wed	20 Tir (Day 113)
Jul-12-2007-Thu	21 Tir (Day 114)
Jul-13-2007-Fri	22 Tir (Day 115)

Jul-14-2007-Sat	23 Tir (Day 116)
Jul-15-2007-Sun	24 Tir (Day 117)
Jul-16-2007-Mon	25 Tir (Day 118)
Jul-17-2007-Tue	26 Tir (Day 119)
Jul-18-2007-Wed	27 Tir (Day 120)
Jul-19-2007-Thu	28 Tir (Day 121)
Jul-20-2007-Fri	29 Tir (Day 122)
Jul-21-2007-Sat	30 Tir (Day 123)
Jul-22-2007-Sun	31 Tir (Day 124)
Jul-23-2007-Mon	**1 Amordad (Day 125) 3745 ZRE**
Jul-24-2007-Tue	2 Amordad (Day 126)
Jul-25-2007-Wed	3 Amordad (Day 127)
Jul-26-2007-Thu	4 Amordad (Day 128)
Jul-27-2007-Fri	5 Amordad (Day 129)
Jul-28-2007-Sat	6 Amordad (Day 130)
Jul-29-2007-Sun	7 Amordad (Day 131)
Jul-30-2007-Mon	8 Amordad (Day 132)
Jul-31-2007-Tue	9 Amordad (Day 133)
Aug-1-2007-Wed	10 Amordad (Day 134)
Aug-2-2007-Thu	11 Amordad (Day 135)
Aug-3-2007-Fri	12 Amordad (Day 136)
Aug-4-2007-Sat	13 Amordad (Day 137)
Aug-5-2007-Sun	14 Amordad (Day 138)
Aug-6-2007-Mon	15 Amordad (Day 139)
Aug-7-2007-Tue	16 Amordad (Day 140)
Aug-8-2007-Wed	17 Amordad (Day 141)
Aug-9-2007-Thu	18 Amordad (Day 142)
Aug-10-2007-Fri	19 Amordad (Day 143)
Aug-11-2007-Sat	20 Amordad (Day 144)
Aug-12-2007-Sun	21 Amordad (Day 145)
Aug-13-2007-Mon	22 Amordad (Day 146)
Aug-14-2007-Tue	23 Amordad (Day 147)
Aug-15-2007-Wed	24 Amordad (Day 148)
Aug-16-2007-Thu	25 Amordad (Day 149)
Aug-17-2007-Fri	26 Amordad (Day 150)
Aug-18-2007-Sat	27 Amordad (Day 151)
Aug-19-2007-Sun	28 Amordad (Day 152)
Aug-20-2007-Mon	29 Amordad (Day 153)
Aug-21-2007-Tue	30 Amordad (Day 154)
Aug-22-2007-Wed	31 Amordad (Day 155)
Aug-23-2007-Thu	**1 Shahrivar (Day 156) 3745 ZRE**
Aug-24-2007-Fri	2 Shahrivar (Day 157)

Aug-25-2007-Sat	3 Shahrivar (Day 158)
Aug-26-2007-Sun	4 Shahrivar (Day 159)
Aug-27-2007-Mon	5 Shahrivar (Day 160)
Aug-28-2007-Tue	6 Shahrivar (Day 161)
Aug-29-2007-Wed	7 Shahrivar (Day 162)
Aug-30-2007-Thu	8 Shahrivar (Day 163)
Aug-31-2007-Fri	9 Shahrivar (Day 164)
Sep-1-2007-Sat	10 Shahrivar (Day 165)
Sep-2-2007-Sun	11 Shahrivar (Day 166)
Sep-3-2007-Mon	12 Shahrivar (Day 167)
Sep-4-2007-Tue	13 Shahrivar (Day 168)
Sep-5-2007-Wed	14 Shahrivar (Day 169)
Sep-6-2007-Thu	15 Shahrivar (Day 170)
Sep-7-2007-Fri	16 Shahrivar (Day 171)
Sep-8-2007-Sat	17 Shahrivar (Day 172)
Sep-9-2007-Sun	18 Shahrivar (Day 173)
Sep-10-2007-Mon	19 Shahrivar (Day 174)
Sep-11-2007-Tue	20 Shahrivar (Day 175)
Sep-12-2007-Wed	21 Shahrivar (Day 176)
Sep-13-2007-Thu	22 Shahrivar (Day 177)
Sep-14-2007-Fri	23 Shahrivar (Day 178)
Sep-15-2007-Sat	24 Shahrivar (Day 179)
Sep-16-2007-Sun	25 Shahrivar (Day 180)
Sep-17-2007-Mon	26 Shahrivar (Day 181)
Sep-18-2007-Tue	27 Shahrivar (Day 182)
Sep-19-2007-Wed	28 Shahrivar (Day 183)
Sep-20-2007-Thu	29 Shahrivar (Day 184)
Sep-21-2007-Fri	30 Shahrivar (Day 185)
Sep-22-2007-Sat	31 Shahrivar (Day 186)
Sep-23-2007-Sun	**1 Mehr (Day 187) 3745 ZRE**
Sep-24-2007-Mon	2 Mehr (Day 188)
Sep-25-2007-Tue	3 Mehr (Day 189)
Sep-26-2007-Wed	4 Mehr (Day 190)
Sep-27-2007-Thu	5 Mehr (Day 191)
Sep-28-2007-Fri	6 Mehr (Day 192)
Sep-29-2007-Sat	7 Mehr (Day 193)
Sep-30-2007-Sun	8 Mehr (Day 194)
Oct-1-2007-Mon	9 Mehr (Day 195)
Oct-2-2007-Tue	10 Mehr (Day 196)
Oct-3-2007-Wed	11 Mehr (Day 197)
Oct-4-2007-Thu	12 Mehr (Day 198)
Oct-5-2007-Fri	13 Mehr (Day 199)

Oct-6-2007-Sat	14 Mehr (Day 200)
Oct-7-2007-Sun	15 Mehr (Day 201)
Oct-8-2007-Mon	16 Mehr (Day 202)
Oct-9-2007-Tue	17 Mehr (Day 203)
Oct-10-2007-Wed	18 Mehr (Day 204)
Oct-11-2007-Thu	19 Mehr (Day 205)
Oct-12-2007-Fri	20 Mehr (Day 206)
Oct-13-2007-Sat	21 Mehr (Day 207)
Oct-14-2007-Sun	22 Mehr (Day 208)
Oct-15-2007-Mon	23 Mehr (Day 209)
Oct-16-2007-Tue	24 Mehr (Day 210)
Oct-17-2007-Wed	25 Mehr (Day 211)
Oct-18-2007-Thu	26 Mehr (Day 212)
Oct-19-2007-Fri	27 Mehr (Day 213)
Oct-20-2007-Sat	28 Mehr (Day 214)
Oct-21-2007-Sun	29 Mehr (Day 215)
Oct-22-2007-Mon	30 Mehr (Day 216)
Oct-23-2007-Tue	**1 Aban (Day 217) 3745 ZRE**
Oct-24-2007-Wed	2 Aban (Day 218)
Oct-25-2007-Thu	3 Aban (Day 219)
Oct-26-2007-Fri	4 Aban (Day 220)
Oct-27-2007-Sat	5 Aban (Day 221)
Oct-28-2007-Sun	6 Aban (Day 222)
Oct-29-2007-Mon	7 Aban (Day 223)
Oct-30-2007-Tue	8 Aban (Day 224)
Oct-31-2007-Wed	9 Aban (Day 225)
Nov-1-2007-Thu	10 Aban (Day 226)
Nov-2-2007-Fri	11 Aban (Day 227)
Nov-3-2007-Sat	12 Aban (Day 228)
Nov-4-2007-Sun	13 Aban (Day 229)
Nov-5-2007-Mon	14 Aban (Day 230)
Nov-6-2007-Tue	15 Aban (Day 231)
Nov-7-2007-Wed	16 Aban (Day 232)
Nov-8-2007-Thu	17 Aban (Day 233)
Nov-9-2007-Fri	18 Aban (Day 234)
Nov-10-2007-Sat	19 Aban (Day 235)
Nov-11-2007-Sun	20 Aban (Day 236)
Nov-12-2007-Mon	21 Aban (Day 237)
Nov-13-2007-Tue	22 Aban (Day 238)
Nov-14-2007-Wed	23 Aban (Day 239)
Nov-15-2007-Thu	24 Aban (Day 240)
Nov-16-2007-Fri	25 Aban (Day 241)

Nov-17-2007-Sat	26 Aban (Day 242)
Nov-18-2007-Sun	27 Aban (Day 243)
Nov-19-2007-Mon	28 Aban (Day 244)
Nov-20-2007-Tue	29 Aban (Day 245)
Nov-21-2007-Wed	30 Aban (Day 246)
Nov-22-2007-Thu	**1 Azar (Day 247) 3745 ZRE**
Nov-23-2007-Fri	2 Azar (Day 248)
Nov-24-2007-Sat	3 Azar (Day 249)
Nov-25-2007-Sun	4 Azar (Day 250)
Nov-26-2007-Mon	5 Azar (Day 251)
Nov-27-2007-Tue	6 Azar (Day 252)
Nov-28-2007-Wed	7 Azar (Day 253)
Nov-29-2007-Thu	8 Azar (Day 254)
Nov-30-2007-Fri	9 Azar (Day 255)
Dec-1-2007-Sat	10 Azar (Day 256)
Dec-2-2007-Sun	11 Azar (Day 257)
Dec-3-2007-Mon	12 Azar (Day 258)
Dec-4-2007-Tue	13 Azar (Day 259)
Dec-5-2007-Wed	14 Azar (Day 260)
Dec-6-2007-Thu	15 Azar (Day 261)
Dec-7-2007-Fri	16 Azar (Day 262)
Dec-8-2007-Sat	17 Azar (Day 263)
Dec-9-2007-Sun	18 Azar (Day 264)
Dec-10-2007-Mon	19 Azar (Day 265)
Dec-11-2007-Tue	20 Azar (Day 266)
Dec-12-2007-Wed	21 Azar (Day 267)
Dec-13-2007-Thu	22 Azar (Day 268)
Dec-14-2007-Fri	23 Azar (Day 269)
Dec-15-2007-Sat	24 Azar (Day 270)
Dec-16-2007-Sun	25 Azar (Day 271)
Dec-17-2007-Mon	26 Azar (Day 272)
Dec-18-2007-Tue	27 Azar (Day 273)
Dec-19-2007-Wed	28 Azar (Day 274)
Dec-20-2007-Thu	29 Azar (Day 275)
Dec-21-2007-Fri	30 Azar (Day 276)
Dec-22-2007-Sat	**1 Dai (Day 277) 3745 ZRE**
Dec-23-2007-Sun	2 Dai (Day 278)
Dec-24-2007-Mon	3 Dai (Day 279)
Dec-25-2007-Tue	4 Dai (Day 280)
Dec-26-2007-Wed	5 Dai (Day 281)
Dec-27-2007-Thu	6 Dai (Day 282)
Dec-28-2007-Fri	7 Dai (Day 283)

Dec-29-2007-Sat	8 Dai (Day 284)
Dec-30-2007-Sun	9 Dai (Day 285)
Dec-31-2007-Mon	**10 Dai (Day 286) 3745 ZRE**

Calendar year 2008 converted to the Zoroastrian calendar year 3745.

2008 AD	Z. R. E. 3745 - 3746 ZRE
Jan-1-2008-Tue	**11 Dai (Day 287) 3745 ZRE**
Jan-2-2008-Wed	12 Dai (Day 288)
Jan-3-2008-Thu	13 Dai (Day 289)
Jan-4-2008-Fri	14 Dai (Day 290)
Jan-5-2008-Sat	15 Dai (Day 291)
Jan-6-2008-Sun	16 Dai (Day 292)
Jan-7-2008-Mon	17 Dai (Day 293)
Jan-8-2008-Tue	18 Dai (Day 294)
Jan-9-2008-Wed	19 Dai (Day 295)
Jan-10-2008-Thu	20 Dai (Day 296)
Jan-11-2008-Fri	21 Dai (Day 297)
Jan-12-2008-Sat	22 Dai (Day 298)
Jan-13-2008-Sun	23 Dai (Day 299)
Jan-14-2008-Mon	24 Dai (Day 300)
Jan-15-2008-Tue	25 Dai (Day 301)
Jan-16-2008-Wed	26 Dai (Day 302)
Jan-17-2008-Thu	27 Dai (Day 303)
Jan-18-2008-Fri	28 Dai (Day 304)
Jan-19-2008-Sat	29 Dai (Day 305)
Jan-20-2008-Sun	30 Dai (Day 306)
Jan-21-2008-Mon	**1 Bahman (Day 307) 3745 ZRE**
Jan-22-2008-Tue	2 Bahman (Day 308)
Jan-23-2008-Wed	3 Bahman (Day 309)
Jan-24-2008-Thu	4 Bahman (Day 310)
Jan-25-2008-Fri	5 Bahman (Day 311)
Jan-26-2008-Sat	6 Bahman (Day 312)
Jan-27-2008-Sun	7 Bahman (Day 313)
Jan-28-2008-Mon	8 Bahman (Day 314)
Jan-29-2008-Tue	9 Bahman (Day 315)
Jan-30-2008-Wed	10 Bahman (Day 316)
Jan-31-2008-Thu	11 Bahman (Day 317)
Feb-1-2008-Fri	12 Bahman (Day 318)

Feb-2-2008-Sat	13 Bahman (Day 319)
Feb-3-2008-Sun	14 Bahman (Day 320)
Feb-4-2008-Mon	15 Bahman (Day 321)
Feb-5-2008-Tue	16 Bahman (Day 322)
Feb-6-2008-Wed	17 Bahman (Day 323)
Feb-7-2008-Thu	18 Bahman (Day 324)
Feb-8-2008-Fri	19 Bahman (Day 325)
Feb-9-2008-Sat	20 Bahman (Day 326)
Feb-10-2008-Sun	21 Bahman (Day 327)
Feb-11-2008-Mon	22 Bahman (Day 328)
Feb-12-2008-Tue	23 Bahman (Day 329)
Feb-13-2008-Wed	24 Bahman (Day 330)
Feb-14-2008-Thu	25 Bahman (Day 331)
Feb-15-2008-Fri	26 Bahman (Day 332)
Feb-16-2008-Sat	27 Bahman (Day 333)
Feb-17-2008-Sun	28 Bahman (Day 334)
Feb-18-2008-Mon	29 Bahman (Day 335)
Feb-19-2008-Tue	30 Bahman (Day 336)
Feb-20-2008-Wed	**1 Esfand(armaz) (Day 337) 3745 ZRE**
Feb-21-2008-Thu	2 Esfand(armaz) (Day 338)
Feb-22-2008-Fri	3 Esfand(armaz) (Day 339)
Feb-23-2008-Sat	4 Esfand(armaz) (Day 340)
Feb-24-2008-Sun	5 Esfand(armaz) (Day 341)
Feb-25-2008-Mon	6 Esfand(armaz) (Day 342)
Feb-26-2008-Tue	7 Esfand(armaz) (Day 343)
Feb-27-2008-Wed	8 Esfand(armaz) (Day 344)
Feb-28-2008-Thu	9 Esfand(armaz) (Day 345)
Feb-29-2008-Fri	10 Esfand(armaz) (Day 346)
Mar-1-2008-Sat	11 Esfand(armaz) (Day 347)
Mar-2-2008-Sun	12 Esfand(armaz) (Day 348)
Mar-3-2008-Mon	13 Esfand(armaz) (Day 349)
Mar-4-2008-Tue	14 Esfand(armaz) (Day 350)
Mar-5-2008-Wed	15 Esfand(armaz) (Day 351)
Mar-6-2008-Thu	16 Esfand(armaz) (Day 352)
Mar-7-2008-Fri	17 Esfand(armaz) (Day 353)
Mar-8-2008-Sat	18 Esfand(armaz) (Day 354)
Mar-9-2008-Sun	19 Esfand(armaz) (Day 355)
Mar-10-2008-Mon	20 Esfand(armaz) (Day 356)
Mar-11-2008-Tue	21 Esfand(armaz) (Day 357)
Mar-12-2008-Wed	22 Esfand(armaz) (Day 358)
Mar-13-2008-Thu	23 Esfand(armaz) (Day 359)
Mar-14-2008-Fri	24 Esfand(armaz) (Day 360)
Mar-15-2008-Sat	25 Esfand(armaz) (Day 361)

Mar-16-2008-Sun	26 Esfand(armaz) (Day 362)
Mar-17-2008-Mon	27 Esfand(armaz) (Day 363)
Mar-18-2008-Tue	28 Esfand(armaz) (Day 364)
Mar-19-2008-Wed	29 Esfand(armaz) (Day 365)
Mar-20-2008-Thu	30 Esfand(armaz) (Day 366)
Mar-21-2008-Fri	**1 Farvardeen(Day 1) 3746 ZRE**
Mar-22-2008-Sat	2 Farvardeen(Day 2)
Mar-23-2008-Sun	3 Farvardeen(Day 3)
Mar-24-2008-Mon	4 Farvardeen(Day 4)
Mar-25-2008-Tue	5 Farvardeen(Day 5)
Mar-26-2008-Wed	6 Farvardeen(Day 6)
Mar-27-2008-Thu	7 Farvardeen(Day 7)
Mar-28-2008-Fri	8 Farvardeen(Day 8)
Mar-29-2008-Sat	9 Farvardeen(Day 9)
Mar-30-2008-Sun	10 Farvardeen(Day 10)
Mar-31-2008-Mon	11 Farvardeen(Day 11)
Apr-1-2008-Tue	12 Farvardeen(Day 12)
Apr-2-2008-Wed	13 Farvardeen(Day 13)
Apr-3-2008-Thu	14 Farvardeen(Day 14)
Apr-4-2008-Fri	15 Farvardeen(Day 15)
Apr-5-2008-Sat	16 Farvardeen(Day 16)
Apr-6-2008-Sun	17 Farvardeen(Day 17)
Apr-7-2008-Mon	18 Farvardeen(Day 18)
Apr-8-2008-Tue	19 Farvardeen(Day 19)
Apr-9-2008-Wed	20 Farvardeen(Day 20)
Apr-10-2008-Thu	21 Farvardeen(Day 21)
Apr-11-2008-Fri	22 Farvardeen(Day 22)
Apr-12-2008-Sat	23 Farvardeen(Day 23)
Apr-13-2008-Sun	24 Farvardeen(Day 24)
Apr-14-2008-Mon	25 Farvardeen(Day 25)
Apr-15-2008-Tue	26 Farvardeen(Day 26)
Apr-16-2008-Wed	27 Farvardeen(Day 27)
Apr-17-2008-Thu	28 Farvardeen(Day 28)
Apr-18-2008-Fri	29 Farvardeen(Day 29)
Apr-19-2008-Sat	30 Farvardeen(Day 30)
Apr-20-2008-Sun	31 Farvardeen(Day 31)
Apr-21-2008-Mon	**1 Ardibehesht (Day 32) 3746 ZRE**
Apr-22-2008-Tue	2 Ardibehesht (Day 33)
Apr-23-2008-Wed	3 Ardibehesht (Day 34)
Apr-24-2008-Thu	4 Ardibehesht (Day 35)
Apr-25-2008-Fri	5 Ardibehesht (Day 36)
Apr-26-2008-Sat	6 Ardibehesht (Day 37)
Apr-27-2008-Sun	7 Ardibehesht (Day 38)

Apr-28-2008-Mon	8 Ardibehesht (Day 39)
Apr-29-2008-Tue	9 Ardibehesht (Day 40)
Apr-30-2008-Wed	10 Ardibehesht (Day 41)
May-1-2008-Thu	11 Ardibehesht (Day 42)
May-2-2008-Fri	12 Ardibehesht (Day 43)
May-3-2008-Sat	13 Ardibehesht (Day 44)
May-4-2008-Sun	14 Ardibehesht (Day 45)
May-5-2008-Mon	15 Ardibehesht (Day 46)
May-6-2008-Tue	16 Ardibehesht (Day 47)
May-7-2008-Wed	17 Ardibehesht (Day 48)
May-8-2008-Thu	18 Ardibehesht (Day 49)
May-9-2008-Fri	19 Ardibehesht (Day 50)
May-10-2008-Sat	20 Ardibehesht (Day 51)
May-11-2008-Sun	21 Ardibehesht (Day 52)
May-12-2008-Mon	22 Ardibehesht (Day 53)
May-13-2008-Tue	23 Ardibehesht (Day 54)
May-14-2008-Wed	24 Ardibehesht (Day 55)
May-15-2008-Thu	25 Ardibehesht (Day 56)
May-16-2008-Fri	26 Ardibehesht (Day 57)
May-17-2008-Sat	27 Ardibehesht (Day 58)
May-18-2008-Sun	28 Ardibehesht (Day 59)
May-19-2008-Mon	29 Ardibehesht (Day 60)
May-20-2008-Tue	30 Ardibehesht (Day 61)
May-21-2008-Wed	31 Ardibehesht (Day 62)
May-22-2008-Thu	**1 Khordad (Day 63) 3746 ZRE**
May-23-2008-Fri	2 Khordad (Day 64)
May-24-2008-Sat	3 Khordad (Day 65)
May-25-2008-Sun	4 Khordad (Day 66)
May-26-2008-Mon	5 Khordad (Day 67)
May-27-2008-Tue	6 Khordad (Day 68)
May-28-2008-Wed	7 Khordad (Day 69)
May-29-2008-Thu	8 Khordad (Day 70)
May-30-2008-Fri	9 Khordad (Day 71)
May-31-2008-Sat	10 Khordad (Day 72)
Jun-1-2008-Sun	11 Khordad (Day 73)
Jun-2-2008-Mon	12 Khordad (Day 74)
Jun-3-2008-Tue	13 Khordad (Day 75)
Jun-4-2008-Wed	14 Khordad (Day 76)
Jun-5-2008-Thu	15 Khordad (Day 77)
Jun-6-2008-Fri	16 Khordad (Day 78)
Jun-7-2008-Sat	17 Khordad (Day 79)
Jun-8-2008-Sun	18 Khordad (Day 80)
Jun-9-2008-Mon	19 Khordad (Day 81)

Jun-10-2008-Tue	20 Khordad (Day 82)
Jun-11-2008-Wed	21 Khordad (Day 83)
Jun-12-2008-Thu	22 Khordad (Day 84)
Jun-13-2008-Fri	23 Khordad (Day 85)
Jun-14-2008-Sat	24 Khordad (Day 86)
Jun-15-2008-Sun	25 Khordad (Day 87)
Jun-16-2008-Mon	26 Khordad (Day 88)
Jun-17-2008-Tue	27 Khordad (Day 89)
Jun-18-2008-Wed	28 Khordad (Day 90)
Jun-19-2008-Thu	29 Khordad (Day 91)
Jun-20-2008-Fri	30 Khordad (Day 92)
Jun-21-2008-Sat	31 Khordad (Day 93)
Jun-22-2008-Sun	**1 Tir (Day 94) 3746 ZRE**
Jun-23-2008-Mon	2 Tir (Day 95)
Jun-24-2008-Tue	3 Tir (Day 96)
Jun-25-2008-Wed	4 Tir (Day 97)
Jun-26-2008-Thu	5 Tir (Day 98)
Jun-27-2008-Fri	6 Tir (Day 99)
Jun-28-2008-Sat	7 Tir (Day 100)
Jun-29-2008-Sun	8 Tir (Day 101)
Jun-30-2008-Mon	9 Tir (Day 102)
Jul-1-2008-Tue	10 Tir (Day 103)
Jul-2-2008-Wed	11 Tir (Day 104)
Jul-3-2008-Thu	12 Tir (Day 105)
Jul-4-2008-Fri	13 Tir (Day 106)
Jul-5-2008-Sat	14 Tir (Day 107)
Jul-6-2008-Sun	15 Tir (Day 108)
Jul-7-2008-Mon	16 Tir (Day 109)
Jul-8-2008-Tue	17 Tir (Day 110)
Jul-9-2008-Wed	18 Tir (Day 111)
Jul-10-2008-Thu	19 Tir (Day 112)
Jul-11-2008-Fri	20 Tir (Day 113)
Jul-12-2008-Sat	21 Tir (Day 114)
Jul-13-2008-Sun	22 Tir (Day 115)
Jul-14-2008-Mon	23 Tir (Day 116)
Jul-15-2008-Tue	24 Tir (Day 117)
Jul-16-2008-Wed	25 Tir (Day 118)
Jul-17-2008-Thu	26 Tir (Day 119)
Jul-18-2008-Fri	27 Tir (Day 120)
Jul-19-2008-Sat	28 Tir (Day 121)
Jul-20-2008-Sun	29 Tir (Day 122)
Jul-21-2008-Mon	30 Tir (Day 123)
Jul-22-2008-Tue	31 Tir (Day 124)

Jul-23-2008-Wed	**1 Amordad (Day 125) 3746 ZRE**
Jul-24-2008-Thu	2 Amordad (Day 126)
Jul-25-2008-Fri	3 Amordad (Day 127)
Jul-26-2008-Sat	4 Amordad (Day 128)
Jul-27-2008-Sun	5 Amordad (Day 129)
Jul-28-2008-Mon	6 Amordad (Day 130)
Jul-29-2008-Tue	7 Amordad (Day 131)
Jul-30-2008-Wed	8 Amordad (Day 132)
Jul-31-2008-Thu	9 Amordad (Day 133)
Aug-1-2008-Fri	10 Amordad (Day 134)
Aug-2-2008-Sat	11 Amordad (Day 135)
Aug-3-2008-Sun	12 Amordad (Day 136)
Aug-4-2008-Mon	13 Amordad (Day 137)
Aug-5-2008-Tue	14 Amordad (Day 138)
Aug-6-2008-Wed	15 Amordad (Day 139)
Aug-7-2008-Thu	16 Amordad (Day 140)
Aug-8-2008-Fri	17 Amordad (Day 141)
Aug-9-2008-Sat	18 Amordad (Day 142)
Aug-10-2008-Sun	19 Amordad (Day 143)
Aug-11-2008-Mon	20 Amordad (Day 144)
Aug-12-2008-Tue	21 Amordad (Day 145)
Aug-13-2008-Wed	22 Amordad (Day 146)
Aug-14-2008-Thu	23 Amordad (Day 147)
Aug-15-2008-Fri	24 Amordad (Day 148)
Aug-16-2008-Sat	25 Amordad (Day 149)
Aug-17-2008-Sun	26 Amordad (Day 150)
Aug-18-2008-Mon	27 Amordad (Day 151)
Aug-19-2008-Tue	28 Amordad (Day 152)
Aug-20-2008-Wed	29 Amordad (Day 153)
Aug-21-2008-Thu	30 Amordad (Day 154)
Aug-22-2008-Fri	31 Amordad (Day 155)
Aug-23-2008-Sat	**1 Shahrivar (Day 156) 3746 ZRE**
Aug-24-2008-Sun	2 Shahrivar (Day 157)
Aug-25-2008-Mon	3 Shahrivar (Day 158)
Aug-26-2008-Tue	4 Shahrivar (Day 159)
Aug-27-2008-Wed	5 Shahrivar (Day 160)
Aug-28-2008-Thu	6 Shahrivar (Day 161)
Aug-29-2008-Fri	7 Shahrivar (Day 162)
Aug-30-2008-Sat	8 Shahrivar (Day 163)
Aug-31-2008-Sun	9 Shahrivar (Day 164)
Sep-1-2008-Mon	10 Shahrivar (Day 165)
Sep-2-2008-Tue	11 Shahrivar (Day 166)
Sep-3-2008-Wed	12 Shahrivar (Day 167)

Sep-4-2008-Thu	13 Shahrivar (Day 168)
Sep-5-2008-Fri	14 Shahrivar (Day 169)
Sep-6-2008-Sat	15 Shahrivar (Day 170)
Sep-7-2008-Sun	16 Shahrivar (Day 171)
Sep-8-2008-Mon	17 Shahrivar (Day 172)
Sep-9-2008-Tue	18 Shahrivar (Day 173)
Sep-10-2008-Wed	19 Shahrivar (Day 174)
Sep-11-2008-Thu	20 Shahrivar (Day 175)
Sep-12-2008-Fri	21 Shahrivar (Day 176)
Sep-13-2008-Sat	22 Shahrivar (Day 177)
Sep-14-2008-Sun	23 Shahrivar (Day 178)
Sep-15-2008-Mon	24 Shahrivar (Day 179)
Sep-16-2008-Tue	25 Shahrivar (Day 180)
Sep-17-2008-Wed	26 Shahrivar (Day 181)
Sep-18-2008-Thu	27 Shahrivar (Day 182)
Sep-19-2008-Fri	28 Shahrivar (Day 183)
Sep-20-2008-Sat	29 Shahrivar (Day 184)
Sep-21-2008-Sun	30 Shahrivar (Day 185)
Sep-22-2008-Mon	31 Shahrivar (Day 186)
Sep-23-2008-Tue	**1 Mehr (Day 187) 3746 ZRE**
Sep-24-2008-Wed	2 Mehr (Day 188)
Sep-25-2008-Thu	3 Mehr (Day 189)
Sep-26-2008-Fri	4 Mehr (Day 190)
Sep-27-2008-Sat	5 Mehr (Day 191)
Sep-28-2008-Sun	6 Mehr (Day 192)
Sep-29-2008-Mon	7 Mehr (Day 193)
Sep-30-2008-Tue	8 Mehr (Day 194)
Oct-1-2008-Wed	9 Mehr (Day 195)
Oct-2-2008-Thu	10 Mehr (Day 196)
Oct-3-2008-Fri	11 Mehr (Day 197)
Oct-4-2008-Sat	12 Mehr (Day 198)
Oct-5-2008-Sun	13 Mehr (Day 199)
Oct-6-2008-Mon	14 Mehr (Day 200)
Oct-7-2008-Tue	15 Mehr (Day 201)
Oct-8-2008-Wed	16 Mehr (Day 202)
Oct-9-2008-Thu	17 Mehr (Day 203)
Oct-10-2008-Fri	18 Mehr (Day 204)
Oct-11-2008-Sat	19 Mehr (Day 205)
Oct-12-2008-Sun	20 Mehr (Day 206)
Oct-13-2008-Mon	21 Mehr (Day 207)
Oct-14-2008-Tue	22 Mehr (Day 208)
Oct-15-2008-Wed	23 Mehr (Day 209)
Oct-16-2008-Thu	24 Mehr (Day 210)

Oct-17-2008-Fri	25 Mehr (Day 211)
Oct-18-2008-Sat	26 Mehr (Day 212)
Oct-19-2008-Sun	27 Mehr (Day 213)
Oct-20-2008-Mon	28 Mehr (Day 214)
Oct-21-2008-Tue	29 Mehr (Day 215)
Oct-22-2008-Wed	30 Mehr (Day 216)
Oct-23-2008-Thu	**1 Aban (Day 217) 3746 ZRE**
Oct-24-2008-Fri	2 Aban (Day 218)
Oct-25-2008-Sat	3 Aban (Day 219)
Oct-26-2008-Sun	4 Aban (Day 220)
Oct-27-2008-Mon	5 Aban (Day 221)
Oct-28-2008-Tue	6 Aban (Day 222)
Oct-29-2008-Wed	7 Aban (Day 223)
Oct-30-2008-Thu	8 Aban (Day 224)
Oct-31-2008-Fri	9 Aban (Day 225)
Nov-1-2008-Sat	10 Aban (Day 226)
Nov-2-2008-Sun	11 Aban (Day 227)
Nov-3-2008-Mon	12 Aban (Day 228)
Nov-4-2008-Tue	13 Aban (Day 229)
Nov-5-2008-Wed	14 Aban (Day 230)
Nov-6-2008-Thu	15 Aban (Day 231)
Nov-7-2008-Fri	16 Aban (Day 232)
Nov-8-2008-Sat	17 Aban (Day 233)
Nov-9-2008-Sun	18 Aban (Day 234)
Nov-10-2008-Mon	19 Aban (Day 235)
Nov-11-2008-Tue	20 Aban (Day 236)
Nov-12-2008-Wed	21 Aban (Day 237)
Nov-13-2008-Thu	22 Aban (Day 238)
Nov-14-2008-Fri	23 Aban (Day 239)
Nov-15-2008-Sat	24 Aban (Day 240)
Nov-16-2008-Sun	25 Aban (Day 241)
Nov-17-2008-Mon	26 Aban (Day 242)
Nov-18-2008-Tue	27 Aban (Day 243)
Nov-19-2008-Wed	28 Aban (Day 244)
Nov-20-2008-Thu	29 Aban (Day 245)
Nov-21-2008-Fri	30 Aban (Day 246)
Nov-22-2008-Sat	**1 Azar (Day 247) 3746 ZRE**
Nov-23-2008-Sun	2 Azar (Day 248)
Nov-24-2008-Mon	3 Azar (Day 249)
Nov-25-2008-Tue	4 Azar (Day 250)
Nov-26-2008-Wed	5 Azar (Day 251)
Nov-27-2008-Thu	6 Azar (Day 252)
Nov-28-2008-Fri	7 Azar (Day 253)

Nov-29-2008-Sat	8 Azar (Day 254)
Nov-30-2008-Sun	9 Azar (Day 255)
Dec-1-2008-Mon	10 Azar (Day 256)
Dec-2-2008-Tue	11 Azar (Day 257)
Dec-3-2008-Wed	12 Azar (Day 258)
Dec-4-2008-Thu	13 Azar (Day 259)
Dec-5-2008-Fri	14 Azar (Day 260)
Dec-6-2008-Sat	15 Azar (Day 261)
Dec-7-2008-Sun	16 Azar (Day 262)
Dec-8-2008-Mon	17 Azar (Day 263)
Dec-9-2008-Tue	18 Azar (Day 264)
Dec-10-2008-Wed	19 Azar (Day 265)
Dec-11-2008-Thu	20 Azar (Day 266)
Dec-12-2008-Fri	21 Azar (Day 267)
Dec-13-2008-Sat	22 Azar (Day 268)
Dec-14-2008-Sun	23 Azar (Day 269)
Dec-15-2008-Mon	24 Azar (Day 270)
Dec-16-2008-Tue	25 Azar (Day 271)
Dec-17-2008-Wed	26 Azar (Day 272)
Dec-18-2008-Thu	27 Azar (Day 273)
Dec-19-2008-Fri	28 Azar (Day 274)
Dec-20-2008-Sat	29 Azar (Day 275)
Dec-21-2008-Sun	30 Azar (Day 276)
Dec-22-2008-Mon	**1 Dai (Day 277) 3746 ZRE**
Dec-23-2008-Tue	2 Dai (Day 278)
Dec-24-2008-Wed	3 Dai (Day 279)
Dec-25-2008-Thu	4 Dai (Day 280)
Dec-26-2008-Fri	5 Dai (Day 281)
Dec-27-2008-Sat	6 Dai (Day 282)
Dec-28-2008-Sun	7 Dai (Day 283)
Dec-29-2008-Mon	8 Dai (Day 284)
Dec-30-2008-Tue	9 Dai (Day 285)
Dec-31-2008-Wed	**10 Dai (Day 286) 3746 ZRE**

Printed in the United Kingdom
by Lightning Source UK Ltd.
112019UKS00001B/82-114